the
anxiety
book

Elisa Black completed her post-graduate studies at the University of South Australia and went on to work in newspapers and magazines in both Brisbane and Adelaide. As a feature writer, entertainment reporter and the health and family reporter for a weekend paper, she has spent the last decade writing about what interests and impacts Australians' daily lives.

In March 2015, Elisa wrote an article about her lifelong struggle with anxiety; it has resonated with hundreds of thousands of Australian readers and inspired her to write this, her first book.

Elisa lives in Adelaide with her husband and two sons.

To find out more, visit her website or follow her on Facebook:

agoraphobicsguide.com
facebook.com/TheAnxietyBook

ELISA BLACK

the anxiety book

*A true story of phobias,
flashbacks and freak-outs,
and how I got my inner calm back*

 hachette
AUSTRALIA

IMPORTANT NOTE TO READERS: Although every effort has been made to ensure that the contents of this book are accurate, it must not be treated as a substitute for medical consultation. Always consult a qualified medical practitioner. Neither the author nor the publisher can be held responsible for any loss or claim arising out of the use, or misuse, of the suggestions made or the failure to take advice. Pseudonyms have been used in this book to protect the identity and privacy of people mentioned.

hachette
AUSTRALIA

Published in Australia and New Zealand in 2016
by Hachette Australia
(an imprint of Hachette Australia Pty Limited)
Level 17, 207 Kent Street, Sydney NSW 2000
www.hachette.com.au

10 9 8 7 6 5 4 3 2 1

National Library of Australia
Cataloguing-in-Publication data:

Black, Elisa.
The anxiety book: a true story of phobias, flashbacks and freak-outs, and how I got my inner calm back / Elisa Black.

978 0 7336 3533 5 (pbk.)

Anxiety – Prevention.
Anxiety disorders – Treatment.
Anxiety sensitivity – Treatment.
Self-help techniques.

616.8522

Cover design by Luke Causby/Blue Cork
Cover photograph courtesy of Adobe Stock
Text design by Bookhouse, Sydney
Typeset in 12.75/19.25 pt Adobe Garamond Pro by Bookhouse, Sydney
Printed and bound in Australia by Griffin Press, Adelaide, an Accredited ISO AS/NZS 14001:2009 Environmental Management System printer

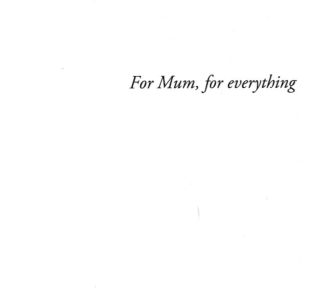

For Mum, for everything

Contents

The first thing I can remember,
fogged around the edges and cast with
the kind of malevolence only decades
of fearful remembering can bring, is
the drowning hole.

1

The drowning hole

Even in the summer sunlight, the side of our house was a sly bog.

Avoided during games of chasey in favour of the sloping cement that ran around the valley-side of our place, it was only during times of great childhood peril – those bored days when we would unchain our bad-tempered snapping terrier and let him chase us around the garden while we shrieked and tried to leap onto the safety of the bonnet of Mum's latest clapped-out car before he latched on to an ankle – that we would sometimes find ourselves forced down the bad side. The dark side.

If we weren't running too fast and the gloom wasn't too deep, we could place our feet carefully on the jumbled rocks that lay between the house and the weed-ferns that no amount of wet could destroy, and make it safely to the back lawn.

But if we misjudged or slipped in the terror-excitement of the chase, we would glug shin-deep into the sucking black muck.

At night, with the heaviness only a day of sunshine and running-climbing can bring, my eyes would droop towards the soft pull of sleep. Then, night-after-night-after-night, I would see my mum and baby brother walking the path down the dark side of the house, would see the depthless hole open up in front of them, and they were unaware they were already dead, their heads sucked under so suddenly and smoothly that not even a bubble of breath would remain, just the dirty-mud surface of the drowning hole.

Most of my memories are of fear.

I wasn't born in a war-zone, wasn't beaten or abused, didn't witness addiction or terrible disease, can't even say I was born with a funny-shaped birthmark or teasable speech impediment. Yet I have a terrible fear that plagued me – that plagues me; that sits in my gut like a mouldering toad or crawls into my chest as a swarm of bees.

Only now do I catch glimpses of what it is to live without it.

The first thing I can remember, fogged around the edges and cast with the kind of malevolence only decades of fearful remembering can bring, is the drowning hole.

Today it reads like some kind of crappy schlock-horror. I'm sitting with my mum and my baby brother on the front lawn of neighbours who live just over the hill. The neighbours' baby toddles in its overalls, fat arms stuck sideways, towards a tiny bridge, while its mum and mine discuss motherly things. And then it topples, face first, into the gaping hole that lies beneath that bridge, and all of a sudden it isn't there any more and its mum is screaming and stumble-racing towards the hole, and I stand there with my mum, who has gathered my brother to her chest, and watch.

I don't remember the baby being pulled from the hole – which Mum insists was only ever a puddle and a shallow one at that – nor do I remember walking back over the hill to our little house for a snack or nap or whatever two-year-olds do on a sunny afternoon.

In my inchoate mind's eye, that baby is dead, the drowning hole an evil entirely capable of moving and feeding on my mum and brother and me, and I must always watch my family and make sure and check-and-check-and-check so they don't die. So I don't die.

As for many children with a talent for the melodramatic, for me the ordinary world sat side by side with the monstrous. For me, much of the ordinary *was* monstrous – sucking, slavering, engulfing, destroying.

The illusory became flesh, tearing at my heels the way our dog would if I mistimed my run around the yard. Childhood anxiety is the gothic horror, the haunting presence, the gaping wound.

When you are young, soft around the edges, malleable and open, everything is 'the most' and the ordinary morphs into horror in a blink – the shadow is the vampire, the creak a faceless ghoul, the parental telling-off is steps away from a *Hansel-and-Gretel*-esque abandonment in the woods.

Of course, now I am grown I no longer fear the drowning hole.

Except that, really, in many ways, I still do.

•

My anxiety is a wild beast.

It has destroyed relationships, clawed at my insides until I was sick, left me cowering under blankets, plagued me with panic attacks and tipped me into postnatal depression following the birth of my first son.

I have taken medication – Aropax, Cipramil, Effexor, Zoloft, to name but a few – tried psychotherapy, hypnosis, exposure therapy, visited psychologists and psychiatrists and naturopaths and herbalists and more.

I've doggedly practised yoga, meditated morning and night, exercised feverishly to try to rid myself of the adrenaline throbbing through my veins.

I've sought solace in alcohol and avoided anxiety-inducing situations to the point of agoraphobia.

Some things have helped for a while, others not at all, and always anxiety was there in some way, lurking around the corner.

For twenty years I have sought a cure and for much of that I haven't even known what I was fighting, haven't understood why I felt the way I did, why I couldn't cope with things others found everyday-normal.

What have I learned?

What wisdom about a life with anxiety – after almost four decades of it – can I impart? Do I know enough to shield my sons, to save the one already feeling the sharp stab of fear in his gut?

Maybe.

This isn't one of those historical mental health books where you will learn all about which psychotherapist developed which treatment in whatever year. When I am in the throes of a panic attack and feel like my heart is about to explode out of my chest, or when anxiety is sending the same thoughts through my head over-and-over-and-over until I feel like I might go insane, I don't actually give a crap when cognitive behavioural therapy was invented or when Zoloft first entered the market.

What I really want to know is that I am not the only one who feels like this, like some strange circus freak who would be laughed at if she ever confessed to the turmoil in her gut. I want to know what might work, how it might work, what else to try if it does nothing at all.

And I want to know what others feel. I want to know about your darkness, your fear, what widens your eyes in the still of the night, or sends you rushing for the toilet in the middle of the day.

For all our differences, the unique reasons why you are you and I am me, there are still universal truths to our terror, a shared knowledge: when you catch a glimpse of your reflection in the story of another and, if even for a moment, you feel less alone.

I want to know that I am not alone, and I want to know the things that might help me get through the next minute, hour, day, the rest of my life. The things that might help you.

•

My anxiety is that tightness in my chest, the wild scrabbling of whatever is masquerading as my heart.

My anxiety is the constant worry, the fixating, the obsessing over things I cannot control: sickness, death, oblivion.

My anxiety is my upset stomach, my inability to focus or sit still or do anything other than lie curled in a ball because the fear is so great I can't even face standing up.

My anxiety says I can't do this, any of it.

My anxiety says life is scary and dangerous and fraught and unpleasant. Even when I am having the most beautiful of days – when I am at the beach with my healthy children, or they are tucked safely in bed and I have a great book and an excellent glass of wine, or I am horse riding or travelling or laughing with my husband, or reminiscing with old friends

– my anxiety is sitting in the corner of my heart, reminding me that this could be the last time I am this happy, that even being happy is dangerous because it is daring the universe to show me how bad things can be, that only by being ever vigilant do I have even the smallest hope of preventing any of those terrible things happening to me or my family.

I am very good at hiding my anxiety. As a kid you learn that being vulnerable is the very best way to make sure other kids know you are weak and easy prey. Never show fear. Never show the bullies that they have made you sad or scared. Develop the perfect poker face. And definitely don't tell others what you are scared of.

Anxious people crave control, perfection, hate being unsure, hate the lack of certainty inherent in life.

The problem with all of this is that accepting vulnerabilities, letting go of control, showing your less-than-perfect face to the world, is part of shedding anxiety like a wrinkled snake's skin.

•

Treatment of anxiety is a movable feast. What works for one person may not work for another, may not work for you or me. And what works for you at one point in your life may stop working and something else may take its place.

And it's important to make it clear – right here at the beginning – that it may be very, very hard to challenge your anxiety. To face your fears. And while it can be hard to see a doctor for the first time, to try a new treatment in the hope that it will be the right one for you, you must persevere. Don't give up if it takes time to find what helps. Don't give up.

People are complex and your anxiety is probably caused by more than one thing. In the same way, you'll probably need to consider more than one thing when it comes to trying to quash it.

And if someone, however well intentioned, tells you to just stop worrying, to choose to be happy – and sooner or later someone will – ignore them, because they have no idea what they are talking about. Anxiety is not something anyone would choose.

But you can choose to try. Try different techniques. Choose, in your calmer moments, to see the funny side of the ludicrous tricks your mind plays on you. Try to accept that, along with all of the truly horrible parts of anxiety, you may also be sensitive, creative, imaginative, funny, caring and all of the other beautiful things that come as the panacea to anxiety. And, more than anything, there is always hope.

Anxiety tries to tell you that the very worst thing could happen at any point, that you need to be always aware, to always keep yourself safe.

Hope tells us that the very best could happen at any time.

It tells us that today could be the day you find your answer.

2

What is anxiety?

Anxiety is the nameless dread that grips your gut and turns your insides to water.

Anxiety is the pain in your chest, the tight ball of gristle squeezing your heart.

Anxiety is the fear that you are dying or going mad, and that everyone will see it happen.

Anxiety is disgust, contamination, dread.

Anxiety is eyes-wide in the small hours of the night, flushing hot beneath the sheets with the terror of the coming day.

Anxiety is sitting in a group of friends and smiling and laughing without hearing a word, so focused are you on just getting through this moment, and the one after, and the one after that.

Anxiety is head-spins, snapping at those you love, the shits, the shakes, tears and tears and tears.

Anxiety is guilt. Guilt for the ruined holidays, the worried parents, the scared children, the frustrated partner ignored or burdened, the opportunities lost, the wonderful marred.

Anxiety is wondering how many more days your body can possibly keep going, feeling as it does.

Anxiety is anger because you can see that life is beautiful but feel powerless to live it without the cloak of fear.

Anxiety is not a worry from time to time, a niggle over something forgotten or mislaid, or a personal slight regretted. It is full-body, overwhelming, life-wrecking, mind-jacking anguish.

Anxiety is too small a word.

•

Everyone feels anxiety sometimes.

The anticipatory nerves you feel before an exam. The edginess that sets you on your toes before a performance. The dread that gnaws at your gut when you are waiting for the doctor to call. Anxiety keeps you safe, helps you perform well, makes you aware, vigilant, ready to react. This is the good anxiety. Well, if not good, then at least helpful.

But when anxiety seeps into every corner of your life, when it colours the days red and fills the dark hours with waking nightmares, when the dread becomes so pervasive that you can't go to the supermarket or see friends or get out of bed – when you fear life itself – anxiety is a problem. More than a problem.

I can't remember a time when I wasn't nervous. Mum called me 'highly strung' and I thought the pressure in my chest must have been caused by strings pulled tight across my body, thrumming and ready to snap.

I wasn't, nor am I now, perpetually panic-stricken; the anxiety ebbs and flows, and often without rhyme or reason. Real-life stress might elicit an appropriate reaction, something everyday might tip me into full-blown panic. Anxiety feeds on itself like a snowball careering down a mountain. The niggles become nudges, the worry becomes anxiety, the nervousness becomes panic and, if you can't find a way to calm yourself, it feels like it might destroy you.

So, what is anxiety and how the hell can we stop it?

You probably already know what I'm going to say next but, sadly, there is no one solution, no therapy or pill guaranteed to cure anxiety in everyone. Anxiety is complex, both in its genesis and its expression.

For every researcher or scientist empirically testing different theories or treatments, examining methods and medications appropriately and thoroughly, there are a dozen shonksters promising a cure if you just follow their seven-step program to develop calm, or sniff this homeopathic remedy made of the distilled tears of anxious virgins.

The worst part is that most of us are so desperate to feel normal, to rid ourselves of anxiety, that we will try just about anything.

When I was twenty-five I went to see a 'doctor' who had a clinic tucked in behind an insurance broker. In his office he attached sensors to my thumbs and had me pick little bottles out of a machine that told him I had contracted glandular fever as a teen (no), had a parasite in my gut (no), and if I went back to see him for at least eight weeks he would be able to cure the panic that was threatening to tip me over the edge. I thought it was bullshit and I went back anyway, so desperate was I to be better.

But solace, relief, might be found – can be found – if you are willing to think laterally, employ multiple techniques, make peace with setbacks and avoid dodgy practitioners who practice BS instead of medicine.

•

Despite the plethora of books written by anxious men, it is actually women who are more likely to be diagnosed with an anxiety disorder.

Perhaps men writing about their anxiety are seen as more interesting, or associated with cooler stuff like attractive vulnerability (as opposed to female neediness) or Woody Allen-esque quirks. The anxiety of women seems to be lumped in with the general 'stuff that makes women women' or as us just being hysterical or on our periods.

There are a few possible reasons why women are diagnosed with anxiety more frequently than men. It could be that we are more susceptible because of our hormonal make-up, that we are just more likely to see a doctor with our symptoms, that the lion's share of childcare falls to us, or that women are more likely to experience gender-based violence, socioeconomic disadvantage, and lesser social status and rank.

The ancient Greeks, although a little confused in their ideas about anxiety (and female anatomy in general – they thought anxiety, mostly observed in young women, was caused by the uterus wandering around the body blocking passages and causing disease), were onto something with the maxim *know thyself.*

A little self-exploration (minus the generally associated wankfest that comes with much self-help) if done with honesty, and a willingness to accept some uncomfortable truths, can reveal where the root, or roots, of your anxiety lies.

Anxiety, in all its clinical manifestations – generalised anxiety disorder, phobias, obsessive-compulsive disorder, post-traumatic stress disorder, panic disorder, among others – is one of the most common groups of psychiatric disorders, seen in around 14 per cent of adult Australians every year.[1]

There is no single trigger, but certain factors may mean you are more at risk: a family history of mental health problems, drug abuse, long-term stress, health issues, even having certain personality traits like perfectionism or low self-esteem.

New research is even exploring whether or not the types of bacteria in your gut could be responsible, and if the poo of an unaffected individual might make you feel better; others are investigating the possibility that postural complaints could lead to panic attacks. Others hypothesise that certain anxious people will benefit greatly from a simple vitamin regimen – but more of that later.

•

If I dwell for too long on the things I fear, if I can't find a distraction or can't reason myself out, my anxiety picks up speed. In many ways it feels like a demonic centrifuge in reverse. As my attention focuses more and more on the 'what-ifs', as I feel more and more overstimulated, inside I feel like everything is spinning faster and faster, the spinning mass's centre getting smaller and smaller and hotter and tighter until it feels like it might either burst from my chest or crush me.

Anxiety, to me, feels selfish. By its very nature it is intro-spective. No matter the source – social anxiety, panic, fear a giant spider will lay human-sized eggs in your shed – the fear is ultimately about what that will mean for you.

I worry desperately about my children – that they will get sick and suffer and die. But the base of that fear, its dark and sordid heart, is the fear of what that would mean for me – what would happen to me if the worst happened to them? I do not think I could go on if they died or were horribly maimed. I do not think I am strong enough.

I don't choose to feel this way. I look at the people around me and wish I could be as unconcerned, as relaxed, as they seem to be. And I understand why anxiety can be frustrating to the people in my life.

I want to comprehend how anxiety seems to others, to those without it. If you haven't been floored by panic attacks or kept awake night-after-long-night with obsessive worry, for weeks and months and years, if you haven't obsessed about your health until you were convinced you were dying and begun to experience the same grief you would if it were actually true, how can you possibly be expected to understand its impact?

Anxiety disorder is just that: a disorder, an illness – and we didn't choose it any more than the person with cancer chooses theirs.

But I get why sometimes others must wonder why we just don't stop.

Everything feels huge and important and slightly unreal when you are small. It's why so many of our demons are formed when we are too young to realise that there really isn't anything to fear in the shadows.

3

Childhood

The drowning hole changed me before I was even fully formed; it coloured my tiny world, populated with plastic horses and books, in shades of fear.

I saw the dreadful in the ordinary. I remember. I remember. I remember lying in my cot, tucked snugly under my blankets, shaking even before the light was turned off and then it was dark and the walls were suddenly glowing in rolling flames. At my scream, Mum would run back and turn on the light, and the flames would vanish, and I didn't know what was real.

Like some kind of shape-shifting swamp monster – the kind found in the library books usually written by Stephen King that I would read in the small hours as a kid and then berate myself for as frothing Saint Bernards and possessed cars kept me awake until dawn – anxiety has loomed large over my life and, with an ancient cunning, changed form as soon as I learned that the drowning hole was nothing to fear, was not even real.

The fear implants itself in your mind, brands itself – charred around the edges – onto your brain. Even though thirty-five years have passed I can taste the mud, still feel the cold edge to the air, see the light shimmering sickly on the drowning hole's oily surface.

And the dread, the fear, the disgust always found something else to inhabit.

At five, in my too-big yellow uniform and clompy brown shoes, I headed off to school, where the teacher tried to engage the tumbling rabble by reading the most gruesome Bible stories, the type most small kids adore.

Of course, while the rest of the class listened in rapture as Miss Spencer told us about Jesus and the lepers, the edges of the room got furry, my heart started popping in my chest, and I was certain that not only did I have leprosy but things were already starting to congeal and blacken and rot.

Catholics have a certain talent for gore which, when teamed with what Mum called my 'chronic imaginitis', left me quaking at my desk, practising my letters with my hands while my mind saw fingers dripping rotting bandages and yellow-cracked nails. I could smell it. Taste it.

While we are often told that kids look to adults for information and guidance, that grown-ups are the keepers of all wisdom, there was absolutely nothing Mum, or any other grown-up, could say that could convince me I was okay.

In the dark of the night I would imagine being forced to a walled-off leper colony, swathed in weeping rags, with bits of fingers falling off in my wake. It wasn't just a fear: it was a certainty. If I didn't have leprosy already – from the browny leaf I accidentally touched or the cat with the smelly breath or from brushing against Sarah Burnett's eczema-leg when we were running away from the squinty boy in Year Six – then it was only a matter of time. I knew this with all the certainty a five-year-old can know anything. I knew it in my bones.

There was some small comfort to be found in the smell of Palmolive soap. If I didn't know if I had touched something 'dirty', if it was safe to reach for the biscuit or to scratch my lip, a quick sniff of my palms was all it took to be reassured that everything was clean and free from contamination. That I wouldn't get sick.

Of course, people looked at me oddly if I did it too often, so I would sniff covertly, would wait until they were distracted; I pretended to bend down to check my shoes and ducked around a corner before cupping my hands and taking the tiniest whiff.

I was a hand-sniffer for years because I was terrified of sickness and thought unclean hands were the fastest way for bugs to breach my outside to make themselves at home in my soft innards.

Germs, however, were not the only thing that scared me, that stirred the anxiety in my chest and sent it surging up my throat.

As a child I also feared – to the point of hysteria – water, vomit, poo, holidays, new food, the devil and jetties. The last meant that, on a bad day, I would wail and dig in my heels if Mum and Dad suggested a walk along the jetty after salty fish and chips on the beach. On a good day I would nod in agreement but stick to the side, holding hand-over-hand to the railing and making sure I did not step on any cracks that might suck me right through into the depthless water underneath.

But dirt, disease and contamination were always the worst, the bringers of nightmares.

Disgust and anxiety are perfect bedfellows, a codependent match made in hell. Disgust – real and otherwise – informed much of my childhood.

I 'remember' being a baby and spewing faeces from my mouth. I 'remember' flames licking the walls around my cot while everyone ran from the front door, not stopping to save the disgusting baby. Neither of these things happened but to me they are as real as the keyboard under my fingers is today.

Disgust was the basis of most of my terrors and fear of death fed all of them, although when you are very small many things appear capable of delivering the mortal blow.

Worse, over time these terrors can morph and grow teeth, and the innocent or absurd can become an eight-foot beast with leprotic limbs that spews mud.

I was two (and what a psychically messed-up year that turned out to have been, with the drowning hole still plaguing my nights) when Mum took my grandpa and me on one of those long-winding cold-weather drives hated by every child.

My grandpa was, quite simply, one of the greatest people in the world. He was the very best kind of grandpa, always wearing his trilby and his professor's coat with the leather elbow patches, brogues and a tie (even if he was just going to the shops), and he smoked a pipe and smelled of tobacco, and on visits would offer us an already-opened bag of Smith's chips tied up with rubber bands and we would eat them even though they were soft around the edges and we didn't much like the crinkled ones anyway, but Grandpa's eyes would twinkle as he gave them to us and we would have walked through fire for that. Soft chips seemed a small sacrifice.

Tall and sprightly, he would make up songs and tap-dance, read me book after book, bring back grown-up gifts like sapphires (and, once, an illicit ivory necklace) from his yearly trips to Harrods that he would give to me secretly so as not to make the other grandkids jealous. I was convinced I was his favourite, although I am suspicious now that that was just the beauty of Grandpa – a man blessed with the gift of making everyone feel the most special.

Grandpa also had anxiety, he'd had a nervous breakdown years before and was wired tightly enough that he would swear 'hellfire bells' in alarm if we tumbled helter-skelter past his armchair, lost in wild 'horseplay'.

On the day of that long drive, finally free of Mum's car, I remember walking on the grass, feet tightly tucked into my gumboots, the reeds of the river in front of me blocking out the far bank, the eucalypts leaning overhead.

Suddenly, from nowhere and now imagined as some kind of sick presage of the fears to come, an enormous black shadow rushed from the reeds and latched firmly onto my boot, dragging me towards the water.

With a roar, Grandpa came charging down the bank and launched a savage kick at the swan – as that is what it was, although it was the size of a man and I swear its eyes were as big as my face. Because it is a memory created in panic and tinged by the colours of family history and decades past, I am unsure how true this next bit is, but I remember the swan was launched in a smooth arc over the gumtrees by Grandpa's brogue and I was scooped up, favourite wellies intact, even if the same could not be said for my sanity.

The damned swan, feathers erect, squawking its snaking skull at me, took on all the importance of family legend and personally apt awkward metaphor – that, for me, even a stupid bird could threaten death.

Everything feels huge and important and slightly unreal when you are small. It's why so many of our demons are formed when we are too young to realise that there really isn't anything to fear in the shadows. When I look back at young-me, with a mixture of sympathy and a desire to shake the child and yell, 'JUST STOP IT AND BE NORMAL' into her pitiful-scared face, I search for the whys of my anxiety; without any grand trauma to blame, beyond the usual scabs and hurt feelings of childhood, I wonder again: *Why why why?*

I always thought we were pretty standard – it's not like we spun our own wool and hoarded canned goods in the shed or had Nazi flags hanging from the porch. It was only when I was old enough to pay attention to the friends who talked about the parties at their houses or weekends spent camping with second cousins or the family friend's kids who were close enough to be considered family too, that I realised something else.

When I was growing up my parents never had people around to our house, only family, and those visits were restricted to birthdays, Christmas or other unavoidable social occasions.

What I wrote off as annoying parental quirks when I was a kid I now see as symptoms of social anxiety. While they could *be* in our little house – Dad giving us horsey-back rides to bed at night or tickling us until we screamed, 'KANGARILLA'; Mum, masked as the Tooth Fairy, leaving me tiny wands made from toothpicks and star-stickers on piles of books instead of the usual coin in a glass, or reading us Enid Blyton books for hours, with impassioned voices for Moon-Face and Silky and the Saucepan Man – in public they were quiet, shy, closed.

As an adult I am a chronic procrastinator who will find any excuse not to do the things that need doing, if I can convince someone else to do it for me (as the anxiety whispers in my ear, 'If you do it wrong, people will think you are ridiculous and stupid, maybe just wait a while'); kid-me was equally – although probably less self-consciously – manipulative. I liked to draw but only if the picture was perfect (how clichéd I was, even then) and would tantrum if it wasn't. But with my half-effort scribble in hand, I would ask Mum what she thought.

With a small-teeth smile she would declare it 'perfect' and 'beautiful', and I would be buoyed (though a little suspicious she might be lying). It is no exaggeration to say that if asked whether I should pull out all my teeth or have horns implanted under my scalp, Mum would say I would look beautiful either way.

Nor does she ever yell. As a vile eleven-year-old, I dodged Mum's farewell kiss on the way to school one morning, not because of anything other than being a feckless pre-teen. When I turned back to see what she was doing, all I saw was a lonely tear rolling down her cheek. That was the first time I had ever seen her cry but, in my childish selfishness, never thought this odd and now felt angry that I was being made to feel guilty. I spent the day making 'sorry' cards covered with enormous blue-texta tears. Mum is the master of emotion-control. While on the inside (although I never knew it) she was terrified of making a fool of herself if she spoke to someone different, on the outside she was calm, self-possessed, almost regal in her ability to keep a half-smile on her face at all times.

My dad was famous among my friends as the 'dad-who-doesn't-speak'. The half-hour school car trip every morning was spent in silence. Dad, like many other Australian dads then and now, spent weekends watching footy and cricket (depending on the season) in silence. When I was in my early twenties and confused about what I should do with my life, he gave me this advice: 'Elisa, no one likes their job. Just get a job at Woolies and you might be able to work your way up to management one day.'

However, he is also the dad who bought me a hat with a feather in it when I got my first job as a journalist, passing it over the table to me with a mumbled congratulations. Unsure what it meant, I asked Mum and she said he had spent hours trawling op shops trying to find the right hat, as he wanted me to know my new job was a real feather in my cap, that he was proud.

He's an enigma, my dad, and I really couldn't tell you with any certainty what goes on in his head. He is a curious man, loves animals and nature, and I like to imagine he would have chosen to be a park ranger or a David Attenborough-esque adventurer if he hadn't been forced to leave school early to help his parents finance the rest of his siblings.

I dreaded the visits to Dad's parents. Their backyard was planted with prickly couch grass that hurt when you ran on it with bare feet, and the corrugated fence radiated brutal heat in the summers. We were never allowed to have a drink when we ate – something to do with getting a tummy ache or being sick on the carpet – and the food was dry and yucky. We forced each swallow down with a grimace.

Beyond the idiosyncratic annoyances kids everywhere find to pick at with their rellies, though, there was more at Nanna and Grandfather's to dislike.

Once in the door Dad would get even quieter, speaking only if spoken to, jolted into answering questions if we were trapped inside the gloomy lounge, where I would trace the designs in the swirly-orange carpet as Grandfather watched cricket and the rest of us sat in awkward silence.

Grandfather liked to tell us about the time he had spent in the army and he spoke to Nanna as if she was one of his troops. Tiny, with fuzzy-curled hair, Nanna spoke softly, if at all, and could usually be found in the kitchen, fetching drinks. On the odd occasions we stayed overnight at their house she would sit up to play poker with us, betting with Vegemite sandwiches. At night my brother Ben and

I would huddle together on their lounge room floor, the house deathly quiet, counting down the seconds until we could leave.

Ben was just three years younger than me, and Nick came along when I was eight. Ben was the willing sidekick, the one decorated with make-up and Mum's skirts, the one who asked for a Cabbage Patch doll for his birthday so I would play with him. If I was feeling particularly mean I would smack him on the head until he snapped, and he would roar and run at me, arms and legs flailing. I would catch him by the front of his head, my arms much longer than his, and he would punch and kick at my stomach while I laughed.

During my childhood, Nick, so much younger than me, was always the baby. He had a bowl cut and was obsessed with *Crocodile Dundee* and *The Young Ones*. At two he would walk around in an Akubra squeaking, 'I'm Mick Dundee', and, 'Oscar Wilde was one of the world's greatest writers, he was known for his homosexuality', in a drawling Neil voice and we thought it was hilarious, would make him say it over and over to relatives and strangers until we were the only ones left laughing.

Funny the things that bind you together, become in-jokes, family lore.

Nick was the baby, coddled, teased; Ben the easy-going middle child, the calm one (unless someone had him by the head, of course). And I was the one with the stories, the 'imaginitis' that ran wild, the nervous energy that sent me running to Mum's legs in fear, the one who saw darkness shadowing the edges of her normal, happy life.

Funny, the roles we are cast in, even then.

4

Disgust

At its most base, disgust is about avoiding disease, something the hypochondriac (*cough*, me, *cough*, but more of that later) knows all too intimately.

To give disgust its due, heightened disgust responses and their associated disease-avoidance behaviours would have been super handy even just last century, before antibiotics and vaccinations became commonplace. If feeling disgusted didn't work (and if you accept that associated useful behavioural variations are inherited by subsequent generations), it wouldn't still be so common today. After all, feeling repulsed by rats might seem pretty redundant now but it could be why your eleventh great-grandmother made it through 1665 without getting the plague.

Researchers have found a correlation between anxiety and disgust: those with disgust sensitivity are more prone to health anxiety, contamination fears and obsessionality.[1]

If you are particularly sensitive to disgust, feel it more easily or intensely than others, you are more likely to have phobias of small animals (especially spiders), eating disorders and female sexual dysfunction (among other things). You are even more prone to superficially unrelated issues like height phobia and separation anxiety.[2]

I remember feeling disgusted by things very early on, and these memories are always extraordinarily detailed. I struggle to describe what I ate for breakfast (maybe porridge, could have been toast – actually, did I have breakfast today?) but can still see the objects on a bookshelf in the back of a room that housed something that made my tummy seize up in horror more than thirty years ago.

Case in point: a trip my family took to Sydney to visit the best man at Mum and Dad's wedding. I was four. Memory is a fickle thing, coloured by our expectations and experiences, and in my mind the best man and his family lived directly under the Sydney Harbour Bridge, which loomed large over their front steps. Obviously bollocks. But I remember being in their backyard, playing with their kids – a couple older, one younger, a boy called Garth who walked around with no pants a lot.

The scratchy grass stopped where the cracked cement began and Garth's potty was set up in the shadow of the Hills Hoist. His older brother – Luke? Lloyd? Leroy? – dared me to take a peek inside. Giggling, I edged towards the potty, sideways tip-toeing, until I could peer over the edge. Curled inside lay a bright green poo. I don't know why but even typing this now gives me goosebumps of horror. Back then, I felt the shiver of disgust race to the top of my spine, where it gathered under my scalp and prickled. LukeLloydLeroy started laughing as I retched and squirmed and ran to find Mum, who couldn't work out why I had even looked in the first place.

So I discovered firsthand what research has since confirmed: a heightened disgust response can start early.

A 2013 study found that disgust propensity can be transmitted inter-generationally – a mother's verbal communication of disgust when she is near her child caused them to display higher levels of disgust and fear.[3]

A 2003 study found a significant relationship between disgust sensitivity and health anxiety, general anxiety and washing compulsions, which are also linked to health anxiety.[4]

So what constitutes an inappropriate response to something 'disgusting' and is there anything that can be done about it?

Graham L. Davey, in his 2011 review, found a strong association between measures of disgust propensity and sensitivity, and measures of hypochondriasis, with strong responses to things like poor hygiene, mucus, faeces and bad breath recorded by researchers.[5]

Disgust was also reported to be associated with more abstract triggers like inferiority and debasement, offensiveness and self-disgust, among others, which is important, as other studies have found self-disgust and shame to be closely related.[6] Experiencing disgust has also been found to make seemingly innocuous or neutral words appear threatening.[7]

There is still some debate among scientists concerning what disgust actually does – what biological advantage it confers – but it is believed that it evolved to protect us from harm. The universal facial response to something disgusting is a wrinkled nose, a turning-down of the corners of the mouth, feelings of nausea and revulsion, fear of contagion, heart-rate deceleration and avoiding the thing you find disgusting, and these may all act to prevent contact with sources of illness, disease and contamination.

There are many advocates for exposure therapy as a good way of dealing with disabling disgust sensitivity but this treatment is very specific – think of the dad who gradually comes to not mind changing his baby's nappy quite so much but who would run retching in the other direction should he be asked to wipe the bottom of a friend. Letting someone sneeze in your face until you are no longer revolted by mucus will do little to change the disgust you feel about vomit or having injections. But repeated exposure to something you find scary or gross can lower anxiety as, over time, anxiety levels drop and your brain has space to realise that there is nothing to fear.

Intensive cognitive behavioural therapy (CBT) has also been found to improve how anxious children react to disgusting stimuli.

CBT works on the theory that our thoughts – not outside events – affect the way we feel. During treatment, negative thoughts are challenged and the way an anxious person behaves during stressful situations is examined.

In a 2015 study, researchers observed the treatment by psychologists of a group of kids with anxiety disorders; they were given specifically tailored CBT weekly for 16–17 weeks. They found that disgust levels decreased following treatment across all anxiety disorders, with the best results seen in kids with obsessive-compulsive disorder (OCD).[8]

Many people with OCD have a handwashing impulse and, for a while as a child, I found I could dim my anxiety if I washed my hands too. A lot. At first it was just around the house, when it was easy for me to run to the bathroom to make sure my hands were clean before lunch, but soon it became a compulsion.

If we were out I couldn't eat unless I could wash my hands first. My hands were contaminated – by god knows what – and the thought of picking up an apple or plucking a chip from a bag and transferring that filth to something that was going into my mouth was impossible.

Sitting on the back seat of the car, slouching despondently with chip bag in hand while my brothers happily stuffed great handfuls into their mouths, I was tortured by a hunger only outweighed by my anxiety.

I doubt Mum knew what she was doing, doubt she knew she was practising a type of exposure therapy, but she would talk me through it from the front seat: *You are fine. Your hands are fine. Take a chip. You will be okay.*

On one car trip, when the crunching next to me got too much, I picked up a chip by its very edge, using just the tips of my nails, and put it in my mouth. I waited for the germs to infect me, waited to be sick. Nothing. I ate another. Eventually the whole bag was fingernail-tweezered into my mouth.

That night I waited for the sickness to come but it never did.

And so it went. Each trip I would become a little bolder, able to eat an apple even though I had touched the skin (after first wiping the apple on my trousers to get rid of any bugs that were only just hanging on), could eat a packed sandwich that had gone sweaty in its box and scared the crap out of me at first but then lost its power when I didn't get sick from that either.

Anxiety isn't eternal; our bodies can't maintain that level of stress for too long, and that is how exposure therapy works. The more often you do something scary and nothing bad happens, or at least it isn't as bad as you feared, the less power the anxiety has, the less likely it is to show up.

•

Disgust is closely tied to spider phobia. As kids (and sometimes now) we would wait until Dad looked relaxed in his chair, possibly with a cup of tea at hand, before pointing madly at his head and yelling, 'SPIDER!!!' Then we'd all laugh as he shot vertically from his seat, swiping madly at his hair and face, glasses knocked sideways.

Dad hates spiders. *Hates* them. Quite often Mum will wake to him scrabbling around in the bed, still asleep, trying to wipe the spiders off her. Harmless grass spiders making their slow way across the lounge room floor are stomped into oblivion before one of us can grab a glass and a bit of paper. I haven't seen a huntsman at their place in years and suspect Dad has squashed them into extinction in their tiny corner of the Adelaide Hills.

Studies into the relationship between spider phobia and disgust have been extraordinarily detailed. The facial expression of people with a spider phobia mimics that of disgust, in the raised upper lip, while people without the phobia don't show the same sneer. But studies of heart rate in spider phobics when they are shown pictures of spiders reveal a response of fear, not disgust. Brain activity in such phobics has been measured and several studies showed greater activation of the amygdala (the area of the brain linked to fear responses and pleasure) towards spider stimuli in phobics compared to non-phobics, but this difference disappeared after exposure therapy. The phobics' brains also showed greater activation of the anterior insular (part of the insular cortex, a brain region between the temporal and parietal lobes that appears to be involved in decision-making, especially when outcomes are uncertain, and the ability to empathise and process disgust, among other things) pre-treatment when compared to non-phobics, and this also disappeared after treatment.[9]

The point of all of this is that if you are like me and find the slimy, the sick and the creeping almost unthinkably revolting, then maybe it is a sensitivity worth exploring, worth testing.

Disgust only holds its power when that very power stays untested, when you don't stretch a tentative fingertip across its boundaries to challenge its worth.

Just eat the bloody chips. Sweep the spider gently outside. Book a trip somewhere tropical and get all the vaccinations, needles be damned. There is nothing to fear here.

5

Epigenetics – the importance of ancestors

The weirdness that is the obvious anxiety of my parents (although Dad would deny it with a shake of his head and then go back to watching the footy) stretches back through the generations.

Mum's side of the family is littered with nervous types, from the mildly anxious to the suicidal, all of us muddling along as best we can, desperately trying to look normal while we indulge in the various routines, compulsions and obsessions that help us feel like we have some kind of control over our anxiety, phobias or depression.

It has long been known that anxiety can be passed down through families but there is no consensus on how.

Some researchers ascribe it to a type of anxiety-prone personality – the perfectionist, the fabulist – as being the likely mechanism.[1] Twin studies support the idea that a genetic cause could be at play, especially in the case of panic disorder, generalised anxiety disorder and post-traumatic stress disorder.[2] Behaviourists suggest that anxiety is a learned behaviour, that negative thought patterns feed on themselves, that the fear of panic makes the panic itself worse, and round and round we go. Some believe childhood trauma is the cause, although not everyone with anxiety will have suffered abuse or major problems.

More recently, studies in epigenetics suggest that trauma or stress suffered – and even the food eaten – by your ancestors could change the way your genes express themselves, could cause one gene to switch 'on' or 'off', making you more prone to anxiety or obesity or many other things.

In other words, the sins of the father really can be delivered on the son.

Recent studies have suggested a link between a father smoking in childhood and his son's chances of being overweight[3]; that smell-memory might be able to be inherited in mice[4]; that what a woman chooses to eat during pregnancy can influence the likelihood that the child will be obese.[5]

When it comes to anxiety, epigenetic research is still – much like my own self-conscious emotional development – in its infancy and yet to show much more than correlation.

A small 2015 study of Holocaust survivors and their offspring found different chemical tags on a gene involved in stress responses compared to control subjects who hadn't experienced the Holocaust.[6]

More mouse studies suggest that stressing newborn mice will increase the stress behaviours of not only their children but up to three succeeding generations of mice.[7]

While I'm no doctor (despite possessing a great stomach for intrusive medical TV), it appears that epigenetics may provide explanations that other familial research does not.

It may explain why your anxiety can be so great that sometimes you can't leave your room or your bed, even though nothing really terrible has ever happened to you, because the fear, faceless and fluid, is there, in your bones.

Why sometimes medication only makes a dent in the physicality of anxiety — the adrenaline dulls slightly, the palpitations settle a little, the obsessive thinking begins to calm — but a correction in chemicals doesn't always equal salvation.

If my genes have been changed because of the true stress suffered by my ancestors, could that explain why anxiety can be so difficult to budge, in much the same way that I can't change the colour of my eyes no matter how many therapists I unburden upon?

My great-great-great-grandpa tried to kill himself many times. Once, in what he must have thought a fail-safe option, by slitting his own throat and then throwing himself off the side of a boat in the bay off Glenelg, South Australia. He survived and was arrested, because attempting suicide was illegal, and if he wasn't already depressed, he certainly became so after that.

In 1889, at age seventeen, following years of abuse and forced prostitution, my great-great-grandmother ended up in the destitute asylum, surely one of the bleakest places in Adelaide, at a time when life in the city was hard and many were suffering from venereal disease and stuck in poor living conditions.

Grandma's great-grandmother killed herself by drinking Lysol, an agonising and slow death, after her brain-damaged son, one of the fifteen children she bore, bashed her with the help of her third husband.

Another relative was sectioned, suffering from 'lunacy'; another tried to throw himself under a horse-drawn tram after racking up debts that left him bankrupt and alone.

My great-aunt Pat, born in that terrifying time before vaccines saved us from many of the worst kinds of illnesses, was struck down with polio as a child. Forever after she was terrified of germs. Never married and an independent 'career woman' before that was even a thing, Pat struck off to Sydney alone, forging ahead despite her fears. But, like many anxious people, she developed different ways of controlling the thing she was most scared of: contamination. She was forever washing her hands and would only pick up things if she was able to cover them with tissue paper first.

While my health anxiety led, in the most sadistic way, to a career as a health reporter, Pat's led her first to study nursing (although she had to quit due to ill health) and then to work as a medical receptionist.

At the end of her life, bedridden in a home, mostly blind and unable to hear, she still refused to see a doctor – someone who could fit a hearing aid or rid her of her cataracts – because he might diagnose something far worse. Even as familiar as her fear is, I want to tell her to stop being so silly; it can be so easy to elevate the importance of my own fear above that of others.

My beloved grandpa had what was then known as a nervous breakdown and was prone to bouts of melancholy.

My grandma, his wife, whose anxiety can be seen in the clasped hands and furrowed brow of every photo taken of her, would suffer from constant nervous attacks that would leave her feeling 'oomi', forcing her to rely heavily on Valium at a time when mental health was neither discussed nor publicly acknowledged.

Mum, whose own battles with social phobia probably add to her great reluctance to ever say anything 'mean', remembers her own health being constantly checked by her mother.

Walking past, Grandma would raise a wrist to Mum's forehead; at the first hint of illness Mum would be packed off to bed and checked upon compulsively. My young sons suffer the same from me. A temperature can be enough to send me off into wild paroxysms of hysteria, imagining every possible catastrophic outcome befalling my bewildered, snotty child.

My anxieties mirror my grandma's so closely, so precisely, that you might wonder whether I had been brainwashed by them, that they'd been repeated so often that they had become my own story. But she died before I turned one.

Anxiety disorders were only given that name in 1980; before then people were written off as hysterical.

Grandma was one of those hysterics. As a five-year-old, and in the fashion of the day, she was taken to a phrenologist who would read her head lumps and bumps and tell her if she was going to be a nurse or housewife, just two of the innumerable options available to a woman in the 1920s.

Instead, he told her that she would eventually contract a serious, long and painful illness that would kill her.

Mum remembers Grandma going to the doctor every weekend to see if she had cancer. Grandma spent her waking hours anxious and fearful, in dread. And that only stopped when she finally really did get sick. An incredibly rare blood disorder, so rare her doctors had never seen it before, found her in her fifties. It would eventually kill her.

And when that happened – when she got seriously sick, when her worst fears were confirmed – she stopped going to the doctor, stopped talking about her health. Stopped worrying.

Now, did she get sick because of the anxiety, because of some weird voodoo with phrenologists and predicting the future, or was it pure coincidence? I'm putting my money on the latter, even though I do have one particularly suspicious head bump in the shape of Ebola . . .

Yet, for a tiny five-year-old to be told by a grown-up that they are going to die a horrible death, that kind of thing that can mark your soul.

When Grandpa first saw Grandma walking down the dust-filled road in a small town on the edges of the desert, he knew he would marry her. She was only seventeen, he was twenty-three, and he knew – *knew* – that she was the one for him. He waited for her to come of age before courting her, knew from that first date that he would ask her to marry him.

Years later, when she sickened, he cared for her. When doctors wanted to put her in care, he kept her at home. When she died, ten years after being diagnosed and just months after I was born (she told Mum she wanted to see me before she went), Grandpa swore there would never be another for him. And there never was.

Despite her fears, phobias, irrationalities, Grandpa loved her.

So could the suffering of my family – the abuse, the hardships, the broken hearts – have twisted the way my genes express themselves, wired me to feel the stab of anxiety more easily so that I might be protected from the pain that befell those who came before me?

If epigenetics possibly holds one of the answers to why so many of us in the safe Western world are consumed by anxiety – every year more than two million Australians will suffer – for me it still isn't a salve for feeling the wretched fool, the cop-out.

For being anxious despite the ease of my life.

Other Stories

Obviously anxiety is not the same for everyone: we all have our prone places, the soft spots easily penetrated and hurt will be different in someone else compared to me. Or maybe not. Maybe you recognise yourself in these tales, or your husband, or your child, or the person you have called your best friend since you were both five years old and found each other in the sandpit on the first day of school.

Or maybe you don't even know that your uncle has terrible anxiety, that the person who sits next to you at work is plagued by panic attacks. So many of us are adept at hiding it. Friends are almost always surprised when they find out I battle it. We think we are protecting ourselves by hiding the darkness, but really we are not: secrecy gives the anxiety power, makes us feel that it is shameful, shows us as weak or stupid.

There is strength to be found in shared stories, in knowing you're not the only one terrified of uncertainty, or illness, or being 'found out'. I once knew a girl who was so scared of mushrooms that she wouldn't even ride in the same car as a pizza that had some in its topping. Everyone has something different about them, even the ones without anxiety.

So I sent a call-out to the people I know to see if anyone would share their stories of anxiety with me, to normalise it, to see how others lived it and, perhaps, conquered it.

The first to respond was M.

Confident, composed, funny and whip-smart, I can't even put a coherent sentence together when he is around, so much do I feel like an uncouth twit. He is successful, worldly and very tall.

And he has anxiety.

I'll do deals with myself all the way to the airport. I have so many rules about what I need to get me through a flight and the list seems to grow each time. If one ritual is missing I think I might lose it. I'll take half a Valium but it never works. I'll buy a magazine I won't read, a new bottle of water that has to be full all the way to the top. I'll ask for a spare seat next to me, or an aisle, or the front row, or the very back. Some seats are 'good', others are definitely 'bad'.

In the end, though, as soon as I board, and the air in the cabin starts to thicken and the overhead lockers close, it always comes, like a volume dial of white noise being turned up.

What does it actually feel like, as we taxi down the runway? I feel like I'm unravelling.

It's a tightness of breath, a tension in my spine, a fear in my heart, sweat on my palms, chaos in my head, turbulence in my body, a sheer panic that my brain is breaking, that catastrophe is nearby, that everybody knows my calamity, a constant clearing of my throat, shift in my seat, a terror that I will lose control, scream and shout and clamour and cry and vomit and shit and bang and run and bring the plane down, make a fool of myself, get arrested, lose my mind, kill myself, hurt other people in this trapped space, with nowhere to go, to escape the terror, and I don't trust myself, or my brain, and I'm convinced this is the time, I'll never be normal again, I won't be able to travel again, live life, do the things I want to do, achieve great things, be alive.

We're in the air now, climbing fast. Am I worried we'll crash? Never. This is about control and I don't have any. I try to read the magazine but the words swim. Do I need another Valium? There's one in my shirt pocket. But then, like water draining from a bath, it begins to subside. The vice around my chest loosens. The crashing surf starts to calm. The seatbelt sign is switched off. I return to normal. But I know the fear will return, too.

Maybe on this flight. Or the next.

I know what he means.

6

Water phobia, tummy aches and ritual

After a while – what felt like a lifetime but was probably only a year or so – the drowning hole of my childhood lost its hold on me, became a faded photo in my mind's eye. But the fear of submersion, being smothered, remained.

I *hated* getting my face wet. Water on my face, in the bath or at the beach, would cause a rapid panicked inhalation followed by much gasping, spluttering and retching, then sobbing.

Mum bought a rubber headpiece that was meant to keep the water off my face when she washed my hair, as without it I would squirm and shriek like a cat when she tipped water over my head. If any water spilled over the edge or trickled between my scalp and the rubber I would feel like I couldn't take a breath and was going to die right next to my palomino

Barbie Dream Horse (movable limbs version) that I had kept in the bath for so long that it had gone mouldy inside, leaking bad-smelling sludge at the beginning of each wash (I loved it anyway). A couple of quick sluices under the surface and it would be okay and, after the torture of hair washing was over, I would (perversely, given my own thoughts about being underwater) plunge the horse under the surface over and over, revelling in the way its blond mane softened in the water before it 'swam' up to talk to Barbie-with-the-hair-cut-off who would be watching keenly from the sidelines.

Hair-washing nights were not the only things to fear.

Sometimes, on those wandering weekends parents are forced to spend with young children when they are desperate to get out of the house but don't have enough money to spend on a film, we would pile into the car and head for the plains.

On the worst of these we would head for the port to watch the ships. Far too scared to go near the edge of the wharf, I dreaded the end of the visit the most when Dad – in the manner of dads who sometimes mistake hysteria for enjoyment or terror as a necessary side effect of toughening up – would drive the car along the dock and make long, sweeping arcs towards the edge and back again.

I would sit, frozen, eyes clamped shut, shaking, waiting for the sickening lurch as the car hit the edge of the pier and tipped sideways into the cold water.

On the drive home Mum pulled those chips from the bag under her legs, passing them back to us kids. While my brothers tore the tops and stuffed smashed handfuls in their mouths, I would watch hungrily but be unable to eat my own. I couldn't let myself eat, the fear felt near the water intensifying and spilling over into the things I could control: the food I put into my mouth. Unless I could wash my hands I would have to wait. I could feel them, the germs, in the creases of my palms, under my nails, in the noxious film coating my skin.

School swimming lessons were agony. In the weeks leading up to them I would cry and fret and have nightmares and picture all of the dreadful things I would be forced to do. I would plan exotic diseases that could befall me the night before, feign agonising stomach pains and headaches and, if all else failed, drop to the floor convulsed with gulping hysterical tears.

Some years this worked – not because my parents ever believed me but, I guess, because it was easier to let me stay happily at home then force me out the door. I was entirely capable of crying and laying on the guilt for weeks at a time, and the discomfort or upset of others was no impediment to my efforts.

Some years, though, they stood strong, and I was forced out the door and crammed onto the bus, where I wouldn't make a scene but, worse, would employ the classic 'no-eye-contact-for-Mum' farewells, certain this would make her feel even more guilty when I drowned and she hadn't even been given a last kiss goodbye.

The swimming centre, like most, was humid with steam and chlorine, and echoed with the thrilled screams of little kids who, implored by teachers to WALK CAREFULLY around the edges of the pool, NOT RUN, would skitter on tiptoes, trying desperately not to break into a trot and be banished to the sweaty plastic seats that lined the edges.

Once in, the children would splash and squeal and completely ignore the impassioned pleading of the overweight swimming teacher, who would become increasingly red-faced as kids dunked and jumped.

I spent as long as I could in the change rooms. I would misplace things in my bag, have to tip it out to find goggles or bathers scrunched into the bottom; my towel would be left on the bus; I would visit the loo countless times. But, unavoidably, I would eventually have to get into the pool.

In a show of support Mum often volunteered as a parent-helper during swimming week, and if I could see her I would shoot drippy agony-eyes in her direction as I sidled down the steps into the shallow end of the pool.

Not wanting to be cast in the same light as Michael Ronenburg, who spent most of each lesson screaming his lungs out while being toted around the shallow end by a pained-looking teacher as the other kids nudged and sniggered,

I had a careful set of techniques planned to avoid putting my face in the water without anybody else noticing.

When the teachers placed hoops under the water for the kids to swim through while picking up rings, I shuffled to the back of the line – by the time the others had completed the activity they were too distracted to notice me puffing along, face held above the water, as I picked the rings off the bottom with my toes, much to the disgust of the teacher, who would sigh and no doubt wonder again why she had chosen a career teaching kids anything.

On particularly horrific days we would be forced to jump into the pool fully dressed and then have to disrobe, without putting our feet on the bottom, until the awful swimming teacher thought we were nude enough to save ourselves should we, inexplicably, find ourselves in the open ocean, fully dressed, and with such an enormous distance to swim that there would be no way we would be able to make it in a pair of khaki culottes.

I was, and am, such a terrible swimmer that were this to happen in real life I would drown no matter how many layers I took off, including skin. While all the other kids shrieked and hooted and pretended to drown as they easily removed their stone-wash denim and swam to the side, I would cheat and put my feet on the bottom as I tugged off my shirt and Michael Ronenburg's screams echoed off the walls.

Straight after dressed-drowning we would practice kayak-drowning. One by one we would sit in a kayak while another teacher who would never be trusted again turned it upside down and then waited for the child in question to escape or panic and tap on the hull to be let out.

Mum thought it would be good to have a quiet word with our teacher, Mr Taylor, the type of man who dressed to impress ten-year-olds and spent most of the day throwing tennis balls at us, and whom we thought irrepressibly cool, to make sure he offered to partner me.

Now deathly scared and humiliated, I slid into the kayak from the side of the pool, in the deep end no less, and let Mr Taylor drag me away from the edge.

'On the count of three. One, two . . .'

And the bastard tipped me over while I was still trying to work out how to take a breath, hold the paddle and clamp my nostrils shut at the same time.

Flailing for the bottom of the kayak, I tapped and was spun around the right way, water streaming from my open mouth and nose, any illusion of coolness destroyed, as Mr Taylor gave me a disgusted look and I knew I would no longer be the recipient of playful classroom tennis ball chucks.

Water phobia is a pretty common affliction and it's thought that many people who have it developed it because of a scary experience with water. Even a questionable one like mine.

Anyway, it's a good idea to try to sort it out so that you don't have to miss out on all the fun things it seems like every other Australian but you is able to do on hot days – which is most of them.

As summer approached I would picture myself, svelte and with sudden-boobs, diving gracefully into a pool, emerging sleek as a seal metres away, where I would take a quiet breath and duck dive back down to swim mermaid-like laps along the bottom. And each summer I would instead flap about on the side while my friends dived and swam and did the kind of underwater handstands I could only dream about. (I still don't know how people do that without their noses being flooded with water until they semi-drown.)

I tried adult swimming lessons, surely one of life's great embarrassments – and, to add insult to grave injury, did them at the same stupid pool where I had tried to learn to swim as a kid.

It smelled exactly the same, was still foggy with chlorine, and there were still annoying kids squealing and swimming laps underwater like it wasn't hard at all.

Starting in the shallow end, which now didn't even reach my hips, the instructor handed me a pockmarked kickboard and told me to start blowing bubbles. I angled my head in the hope that she wouldn't realise I was only blowing them with my mouth and my nose was safely above the surface. I blew some really spectacular bubbles, taking care not to swallow any water (because of poo germs), and looked at her with something resembling pride when I popped back up.

After she had explained that I would need to put my whole face in the water if I ever wanted to swim properly, and I tried and failed to do so without gagging, now with added pathetic-mewling in the back of my throat, she suggested we concentrate on backstroke so at least I might have some hope of saving myself should I ever fall off a boat.

I only went twice because I felt like such an enormous idiot, flailing along spastically while five-year-olds powered by doing explosive butterfly, but I am confident I could save myself should I fall off the side of a boat into the shallow end of a quite-small pool wearing khaki culotttes. And I do feel less anxious about being near water and accept that I am probably never going to be a free diver or be able to swim gracefully along the bottom of a deep pool with my eyes open while wearing one of those mermaid-tail thingos.

Some of the best advice on dealing with water phobia is also, like much that deals with anxiety in general, about bringing in some rational thought to dispel the shadows of dread.

Swimming lessons with a real teacher (not some bossy relative or someone who thinks it is funny but also helpful to slyly dunk you when you least expect it) are a great idea. Let the teacher know that you are freaked out; don't be embarrassed to say you have a water phobia – you won't be the first or last to confess to that.

Nor do you have to go from being someone who is so scared of water that you don't go outside when it is raining to someone who can sit on the bottom of a pool for a minute in your first lesson. You can actually take your time; be patient with yourself: just sit near a pool or dangle your feet in the water if you can.

Be a bit braver each time.

It's an annoying cliché when people say this like it is easy but there is truth in facing your fears. Salvation lies there.

Not that I am any great example of that, having spent a large proportion of my childhood (all right – adulthood too) finding ways to get out of doing things I have no intention of doing. Even if my brain was struggling to find a reason, my body would know in advance when something scary was coming up and find an appropriately disabling response.

While feigned tummy aches were often a ruse to get out of doing something scary, more often than not the aches were real.

I was plagued by stomach pains throughout childhood, the kind that felt like a bladed fist turning somersaults below my belly button. If they happened at the shops, I would stagger along behind Mum, bent double, clutching my sides.

Frequent trips to the doctor turned up nothing nefarious and I was diagnosed with tummy aches of an unknown origin. Mum was told they would probably turn into migraines when I grew up and, eventually, they did.

Mum reckons I mostly complained about tummy aches when I didn't want to go to school and it's entirely possible I bunged on a fake one in the mornings when I wanted to stay home. A girl's gotta use the tools at hand.

But I know that often they were real and scary. If I bent over tightly enough, with my fists wedged against my gut, I could take the edge off enough to be able to talk. I didn't feel sick with them, and (surprisingly for me) didn't associate them with the possibility that I might vomit; they were just a paralysing pain.

Stomach pain with no obvious physical cause is a pretty common complaint of childhood, more often seen in girls and kids in lower-income homes. Multiple studies have found connections between these types of stomach aches and anxiety and depression.

A recent study tracked more than 300 children with stomach pain that had no specific cause (known as functional abdominal pain or FAP). It found that, compared with kids without FAP, the ones with tummy pains were four to five times more likely to have anxiety disorders nine years on. About 50 per cent of them had social anxiety, phobias or other anxiety disorders compared with the 20 per cent who had no pain.[1]

Study researcher Lynn Walker, Professor of Pediatrics at Vanderbilt University in Tennessee, USA, said in an interview with livescience.com that it wasn't the pain itself that was making them anxious, as once the pain went away there was still significant clinical anxiety present.

'We need to address the pain and anxiety together and help kids cope better with their discomfort,' she says.[2]

Kids complaining of tummy aches should be seen by a doctor to make sure there is nothing seriously wrong, but even if nothing sinister is found the pain can still be real.

'We have a natural ability to turn down the pain signal once whatever's wrong has healed, or if there's nothing wrong,' Walker says. 'People who are anxious have more difficulty turning off that alarm system.'[3]

It is hard, though, to work out what came first – the pain or the anxiety. Maybe the pain caused kids to be stressed and more vigilant for other pain, or maybe anxiety makes someone more attuned to otherwise unremarkable bodily sensations.

The study also found that kids with abdominal pain are at an increased risk of depression in adulthood. Happy news all round!

•

Children don't have a lot of power, their circle of influence stretching maybe to the dog, teddies and younger siblings who can be beaten into submission. The fears of childhood are big, wild, and with no obvious weak spots. Kids don't have experience or rationale to wield so control has to be found elsewhere.

Without carriages to throw myself under or ancient super-stitions to obey in exchange for protection, I was instead forced to adopt a set of elaborate rituals to protect myself against the world.

One of my favourite primary school possessions was a poster, souvenired from the *Sunday Mail*, which had the entire cast of *Neighbours* on it pulling stupid faces. Soon I couldn't sleep until I had mimicked every one of those stupid faces, Craig McLachlan's being particularly hard to pull off.

I couldn't say the word 'devil' so had to say 'deveeled' when talking about the eggs so that I wouldn't be possessed.

I had a water-drop-flicking routine in the bath that took more time than washing, my anxiety peaking as I neared the end, fearful I would mess it up or run out of drips and have to start again lest my family be killed in a car crash.

As much as home was filled with terrors like baths and imaginary drowning holes and the perils that inevitably followed ignoring the siren call of the *Neighbours* poster, school camp would cause the most profound homesickness known to humanity.

It's not entirely irrational to feel this way because such camps always seem to be held in winter when you have a cold of some kind, you have to sleep in a dorm with a whole troupe of farty eight-year-olds, someone will spew so there is the floating germ thing, and you will be forced to take part in team-building activities like cooking damper in a wet hole, damper you will have to eat half raw when the rain turns to hail and the class is forced to beat a hasty retreat inside.

On Year Three camp – still probably the romantic pinnacle of my primary school experience – a posse of boys marched into my dorm and tried to present me with a sweaty bag of lolly raspberries and a poster of the native birds of South Australia, borne aloft like the Ark of the Covenant. While it appeared that I was the hot catch among the other eight-year-olds, it is a sad fact that I was unable to appreciate being this desired until I was in my twenties and boys were no longer impressed by my Princess Leia double-bun hair or by the fact that I was really good at high jump. Sadly, at that point in Year Three camp all I could think about was that I had overheard Jarrod Weatherald's mum telling a teacher earlier in the day that he was a bedwetter and about the unfortunate fact that I had scored the bunk below him.

Located far from the objects and safety behaviours I had designed for myself at home, I lay, prone and alone, listening to the slats above me creak as Jarrod rolled over again, shifting my body so I was as far from where he lay as possible, eyes wide in the dark, counting and flicking and jittering with nerves.

Ritualistic behavour is everywhere. From the tennis star who bounces the ball the exact same number of times, tickles his nose and hoicks his shorts before each serve, to the actor who indulges in a series of nonsensical behaviours before stepping on stage, rituals give those who perform them a feeling of being in control.

And it's not just people who do them. A 2011 study published in *Neuroscience and Biobehavioral Reviews* found that almost every human and animal activity can be divided into three parts: preparatory, functional and confirmatory. While the functional needs to be performed in order to complete the task, the other two aren't strictly required, don't have any direct impact. Researchers suggested that pretty much everyone indulges in these kinds of routine but nonessential behaviours to some extent, that they give us a feeling of certainty in face of the uncertain – life. It's just some people, those with anxiety, tend to do them to an obsessive degree.[4]

Like so much with anxiety, ritual only becomes a problem when it negatively affects your life. Knocking on wood if you are near a table when someone says something rash can be written off as a quirk; not being able to rest until you can find a tree to knock on every time someone says something mildly discomforting can not.

Other Stories

A is a girl I used to work with – a young woman, I guess, but calling her a 'woman' (because I am so much older) makes me feel positively ancient. She is beautiful and smart and always looks very together, with smooth hair and white-white teeth. Since we stopped working together I only see her posts on Facebook, always at events, smiling and laughing.

And she has anxiety.

I've never had a panic attack as such but I do get really anxious (sweats, cramps, nausea) leading up to social events and I've found in the past year if I try a breathing technique it calms me and stabilises my blood pressure. I breathe in for seven seconds counting slowly, then exhale for seven seconds and repeat until I feel better.

Exposing yourself to the thing you are scared of, the thing that you would normally avoid, is the best way to go. This is scary, especially if you have spent much of your life avoiding.

7

Avoidance

When I was six I was exceptionally good at playing recorder.

I had a brown recorder with white on the ends and I made sure the mouthpiece was always free of spit, because whenever I stood next to Toby Hills-Spencer his instrument blew old slag in every direction. I did not enjoy standing next to Toby Hills-Spencer.

Recorder was the instrument of choice in 1982 and the kids in my class would treat theirs with wild abandon. At the school bag rack you could see the recorders jammed next to jumpers and lunchboxes, sticking out at odd angles, being banged against the wall; a couple of the more poorly stowed would end up on the ground and then kicked under the shelves, where some unfortunate child would be forced to lie face down on the sticky cement to scrabble wildly with an arm or scavenged stick in an attempt to hook the instrument back out. My recorder never ended up on the ground (if it had I would have had to throw it in a lake – ground contamination and floor germs, et cetera).

At the end-of-year Christmas concert I got to stand in the front, recorder gleaming, as we played 'Silent Night'. I imagined the clarity of my notes could somehow still be heard above the squawking honks of Toby's recorder and Michael Ronenburg's I-DONT-WANT-TO-DO-THIS-MUMMYYYYY wails.

And then, in Year Two, everything changed.

My teacher, Mrs Porter, after having a secret word with Mum, told me I would be moving up a couple of grades for recorder lessons; I would have to play alongside the scary Year Fours.

At my first lesson I sat next to Sarah Simons, my good friend Annabelle's adopted Korean sister. Sarah was cool and very good at recorder, and also very good at covert stink-eye. When I tried to play I could see her peering at me with what I thought was a mixture of horror and disgust.

I couldn't concentrate on the notes to the theme from *Peter Gunn*, my fingers covering the wrong holes. I suddenly noticed every scratch on the mouthpiece where my teeth had accidentally grazed it and felt ill when those marks touched my lips. My recorder honked and I stayed home sick – tummy ache – for the next lesson.

And there ended my recorder career. I refused to go back.

Avoidance is the way I almost always tackle tough or scary situations.

If there is a way out, I will take it. And, in that moment, my anxiety is relieved. I feel better, lighter, glad. But avoidance is a terrible way to deal with anxiety. It makes it worse, intractable.

Quitting recorder may have caused no lasting issues – I can't imagine forging ahead with a recorder-recording career. But I never was brave enough to learn another instrument and it's something I wish I knew, wish I had done.

Avoidance has made me miss out on things I dearly wanted for myself.

There are a few maladaptive (i.e. bad) ways the anxious person tries to rid themselves of anxiety that work in the short term but are crap in the long. While adaptive strategies improve your ability to function, maladaptive do the opposite.

You might be hypervigilant and be ever aware of the things that make you anxious, practising and Googling and obsessing about what will happen if the thing you fear occurs. You might establish a set of safety behaviours that you rely on in order to cope with your anxiety – you can only go to the shops if you have your wife with you, you carry a sick bag 'just in case', you constantly seek reassurance that everything is okay.

But the most common thing the anxious person employs to lessen – at least in the moment – their anxiety is avoidance and because it actually does work (again, *in the moment* it lessens the anxiety) an anxious person is more likely to use the technique again and again and again. The problem is that, without facing their fear, they are never able to learn that they can tolerate that anxiety.

I've done all of these maladaptive behaviours, to varying degrees, over the years but I absolutely rely most on anxiety-avoidance. Anxiety is highly unpleasant – no one enjoys feeling like something bad is going to happen – and I discovered very early that if I avoided what made me feel bad, I didn't feel bad any more.

However, avoiding a stimulus, such as public speaking, can become even more disabling when a person not only avoids the speeches themselves but also avoids thinking about giving one, memories associated with speeches, walking past somewhere a speech was once given.

I did it with the drowning hole, with swimming, with talks at school. I have done it while travelling, when I am scared of getting sick, in relationships.

Basically, I should have done what old people suggest and got 'back on the horse', but I have crippled myself by avoiding the horse for decades. And the grand paradox is that I avoid it because I am scared of what the avoidance has in fact created: a life half lived.

Even procrastination – of which I am a master – is a form of avoidance. If I'm worried that something I do will be judged as lacking (*cough*, this book, *cough*) I will put it off for as long as I can to avoid the possible confirmation of my worst fears.

Of course, like everything, avoidance only becomes a problem when it passes the point of being useful and buggers up your life.

If you are driving in the rain and choose to turn on your headlights and slow down, accidents might be avoided. Brushing your teeth regularly might help you avoid root canal surgery. This is useful and sensible avoidance behaviour. Yet, because most of us are vaguely intelligent beings, we see the success achieved by these types of 'avoidance' behaviours and then some of us try to apply this type of thinking to all possible threats, including thoughts and the mostly uncontrollable vagaries of life.

When you avoid something to escape feeling anxiety, you are cementing the idea that the thing you avoided was dangerous. That means next time you are likely to feel even more anxious when faced with it, so you avoid again, and so on.

Some studies have also shown that people who try to suppress painful or anxiety-triggering thoughts later show an increase in this suppressed thought compared with those people who do not suppress.[1]

There are a few things you can do to stop avoidance, apparently, and they all sound easier said than done:

– Recognise that avoidance doesn't work.
– Think about what avoidance has cost you.
– Learn to tolerate uncomfortable thoughts and feelings.[2]

Much can be achieved with CBT (more on that later) and by simply recognising that you avoid what you fear, that avoidance is damaging, and trying to learn ways to avoid, if you will, avoiding.

•

This confession probably makes me sound like I have sub-par intelligence (and maybe I am so subpar that I don't even know I am subpar) but I didn't realise I was an avoider until I noticed, just a year or two ago, that I was almost literally bathing in hand sanitiser every day ostensibly to avoid sickness and the inevitable visit to the doctor – I was terrified that while giving me pills for my throat infection or sinusitis, this doctor would diagnose me with something unrelated, scary and incurable. The kind of thing he would be able to recognise as soon as I walked into his rooms because of the asymmetry of my face or some odd smell or, even more crazily, a test that was performed on me while I was sleeping by those close to me who are worried about the weird disease symptoms that are obvious to everyone except me. That last worry doesn't arise too often – only when I have spiralled into serious panic attack territory, when the most bizarre and nonsensical scenarios will suddenly begin to make perfect sense.

Avoidance when applied to health anxiety can even bring about the thing that is most feared. If you avoid the doctor to the point of not seeking help with a real problem – the lump in the breast, the strange-coloured mole – you might miss the window of treating it in time.

•

Safety behaviours are ways of partially avoiding scary stuff too. If you have social anxiety you may be able to get to a party but only if you stick to talking to your friends about safe subjects. Or you might get super drunk to dull your nerves. They are more subtle techniques than overt avoidance but they still stop you from feeling the full brunt of the thing you are afraid of and still reinforce that it is something to be scared of. So you might be able to go travelling if you carry medications in your bag 'just in case', which might make you feel more in control but also reinforce in your mind that there is something there to be afraid of and to plan to manage.

Reassurance is another way you might try to stave off anxiety. I do this (I really am a walking anxiety cliché). When my kids are with Mum and I have a moment when my mind can wander, I will sometimes start to stress that they are sick and Mum is about to call me. The thought of the fear I would feel during that call is enough to make me pre-empt with a message of my own – *Are the boys okay?* – and Mum will respond with an *Everyone is fine* and my anxiety will dim for a while. But it will come back eventually. Maybe the next day, maybe just later that afternoon, and I will feel compelled to message again just to numb the anxiety again because I can't stop the thoughts going round and round my head nor the gnawing in my gut.

So, is there a better way to stop them?

There is an acceptance and commitment therapy (ACT) technique called defusion. One way therapists achieve this is by getting an anxious client to repeat, over and over and over, a word or phrase that they find terrifying. For me that might be 'vomit' (*bleurgh*, shudder). It's thought that repeating the word or phrase enough times can remove the literal meaning of the word and just leave the sound. The result, hopefully, is that the meaning attached to the word, the fear that makes you want to flee or avoid, is extinguished, if only temporarily.

Exposing yourself to the thing you are scared of, the thing that you would normally avoid, is the best way to go. This is scary, especially if you have spent much of your life avoiding. It's hard to drop that behaviour, even hard to acknowledge that what you have been doing, although it felt right, has actually made your anxiety harder to live with. That's okay. It's hard being anxious and sometimes you just have to play the best hand you have at the time.

If, however, you can start to expose yourself a bit at a time to the thing you avoid, if you can be with the anxiety even when it feels awful and you fear you might go mad, it *will* lessen.

8

Teen years

There are few things in life worse than being a teenage girl.

Yet while you are one, you will be told, time and again, that these years are the best of your life.

'It's all downhill from here,' your socially awkward neighbour will say the day your mum discovers you have your period and celebrates it by telling your dad and leaving a rose on top of a giant packet of maxi-pads (the old kind you attach with safety pins – god only knows where she found them, had probably bought them the day you were born) by your bed.

'Enjoy the freedom,' Auntie Sharon says as you twist anxiously at the dinner table, forcing down your chewy lamb chops and wet beans, because you need to ring your two best friends to make sure they still like you because teen girls are fickle and can hate you the same day they tell you they throw up all their meals.

'All my best memories are from being a teenager,' Mr Callahan, the maths teacher who wears a brown V-neck jumper with a brown shirt *and* tie and rubs himself on the back of the girls' chairs when looking at their work, says straight after the lunch you spent in the loo crying quiet tears because if one more giggling fourteen-year-old calls you Twin Choc for your 'two stick legs', you might never come back.

Adolescence is a perfect storm of anxiety – the surge in hormones, unpredictable relationships, teenage manipulations and insecurities, the cut and thrust of school dynamics, not being cool enough to be friends with the 'trendies', the cold horror that is periods.

I dedicated many hours of planning and rumination to working out ways to keep my friends, hitting on what I thought was the fail-safe solution.

It began with a subtle hint about something mysterious yet amazing towards the end of the school day, whispered in the ear of Angela or Yvette, the two scariest girls in my friendship group.

This worked at first, especially if followed up with the vague-yet-dramatic post-dinner phone call.

'Oh my god, I can't wait to tell you about what happened,' I would whisper conspiratorially.

'Why don't you just tell me now?'

'Oh, I need to show you something about it. I will at school, probably at lunch.'

'Okay, whatever.'

I would begin to panic at this point, certain Yvette had seen through my (pretty obvious) lies and would desperately hunt around for something else to keep her hooked.

'I forgot, I have something for you too.'

'Oh, wicked, what is it?'

'Hang on, Mum is calling me, I have to go. Save me a seat in English and I'll give it to you then.'

And, hey presto, friendship pretty much guaranteed for at least one more day.

A fear of being socially excluded is fairly standard teenage fare and the reason most fear they will be excluded is because they will be discovered to be different or yucky or not enough. This fear can manifest as shyness or people-pleasing or the kill-or-be-killed mentality – out someone else before they can out you.

It becomes social anxiety or phobia when that extreme shyness or self-consciousness turn into fears that take over your life, that make the usually enjoyable terrifying.

School presentations are a particularly acute teenage terror if you are anxious.

Often able to feign illness and stay home on the day I was due to present, there was still the odd occasion when even my kind and gullible mum could not be convinced that I was deathly ill.

On those days I would spend the hours leading up to the presentation in a panic, unable to talk to friends, until I was finally summoned to the front of the class where I would launch into a mostly unintelligible ramble, speeding through my cards so quickly that what took the allotted five minutes at home was over in a minute in class.

My heart would beat out of my chest, my hands would shake and I would hear giggles and whispers as my face flushed and the teacher told me to slow down.

Eventually, the fear that I would look stupid, that my friends would stop liking me and I would be left alone, turned into a terror of vomiting, that I would do it rapidly and with no warning in the classroom or the bus.

The fear of vomiting – emetophobia – consumed me. It wasn't just a thought; I could see it happening, could see my stomach contract and the vomit force its way through my clenched lips in a violent surge. Worse, I would see the faces of the people who would witness it, the look of disgust on their faces, the way they would nudge the people next to them and point and back off, lips tugged away in horror.

Perversely, I have rarely vomited. Other than the usual baby regurgitations, through all of my school years I threw up just once because of an intractable case of gastro that took out the whole family.

To be so terrified of something that was so unlikely to happen only made my fear of it worse. If I rarely did it, how could I trust myself to see the warning signs?

The only thing that made sense was to stop eating at school. Ravenously hungry, I had a few safe foods – apples, bread, chips – that I thought were free from contamination and therefore unlikely to give me food poisoning.

I washed my hands over and over before touching food, until my hands were dry and sore but clean-clean-clean. After washing my hands I would wait until someone else was leaving the bathroom so I could duck out of the door behind them, not wanting to touch the door because that would mean poo-germs and having to wash all over again.

When I got home from school I would devour the first thing I saw in the fridge, ravenous from a mixture of relief at making it through another day and sheer physical hunger.

Along with the obsessions and compulsions around food – the handwashing, the fear of germs and contamination – I developed a series of rituals to protect the rest of my life.

I kept my dog's hair in a small jar and believed that would keep her and everyone else safe.

Of course, in retrospect, this was nuts, but at the time all signs pointed to this collection being responsible for my life not being ruined – I had a container of dog hair (which in my mind symbolised how much I loved the dog, although I really didn't care much for her and suspected I was trying to convince myself I was a kinder person than I actually was) and everyone in my family was all right. The hair was a kind of totem, a symbol of how much I cared and something I could control in a world of uncertainty and tragedy.

The dog hair collection began when Mum and Dad were packing up the car for one of our interminable annual family holidays to some small east coast town where we would stay in a caravan park or budget hotel, the kind with suspicious smelling coverlets and stained carpet.

Holidays were a source of dread: the break from routine, exposure to the unknown, the unexpected. In the weeks leading up I would fret and try to convince my parents that we shouldn't go – that it would be too hot and there might be a fire and we should stay to protect the house, or that I would get sick in the car. Whatever I thought might change their minds. They never did.

I was paralysed by fears of car crashes and friends finding someone new while I was away and sickness and terror-guilt that the dog would die before I could take her for more walks.

Moments from leaving for this particular holiday, and being a teen with a flair for the dramatic, I grabbed the dog – an unfortunate-looking chihuahua called Katie – and stuck my face into her neck, sobbing. As I patted her, and probably because nobody patted her that often, fistfuls of hair came away in my palm and straightaway I knew that if I kept some of that hair it would mean that I did love the dog and I wasn't a horrible, disgusting person.

That poor dog stuck around for almost fifteen years, although it hadn't started auspiciously for her. She arrived as a present for my tenth birthday and I paraded around the house with her perched on a pillow because she was small and hardly hairy and I didn't really want to touch her and was scared I would hurt her or her dog germs would hurt me.

But at bedtime, suffering from post-birthday exhaustion, I tripped as I went to put her to bed in the laundry and she tipped off the pillow, landing hard on the tiles. Scared she would die but better at avoiding what scares me than facing it, I never told anyone.

Over the years Katie had put up with being routinely ignored in favour of the horse I had begged for and that my parents finally found in the Give Away section of the paper; being yelled at when she got under my feet and avoided in terror when her hips dislocated and I sobbed hysterically because, in my selfishness, I thought it hurt me more than it hurt her, my mum always telling me everything was okay while my dad tried to help the dog back to her feet.

Having quit work as a teacher to stay home and raise us kids, Mum took in ironing to help the family get by, most embarrassingly ironing for the family of a girl the year ahead of me at school whose dad had been on *Sale of the Century*, making her the arbiter of all that was cool.

My first horse – Cowboy, a decrepit grey pony with a hatred for anything living – would pretend to be asleep until I forgot myself and walked behind him, whereby he would launch a ferocious kick at my face, somehow always missing but not for want of trying.

Swiftly passing him on to an unsuspecting family for $100, I found a big bay gelding in a nearby paddock for sale. Mum knew his owner and hurriedly struck up a deal that meant she ironed for them for free – great piles of uniforms and shirts and handkerchiefs, sometimes even sheets – so I could have the bay and join the local pony club.

Pony club was an exercise in coveting. While the other girls and their rich parents arrived in grand horse floats, with mums who kept thermoses of soup in the front footwell of the four-wheel drive for lunch breaks, blond hair bobbed, pearls resting on chambray shirts, feet encased in shiny boots that had never gone near mud, I would hack the 11 kilometres to the grounds, through rain and hail and sleet, feet squelching in my second-hand rubber boots, fingers frozen into grasping claws that would only unclench, hours later, in a hot bath.

Mum would follow in her latest old bomb to make sure I didn't fall off and lie there, with a brain injury and no one to help. We would cower by the bomb under the leaky pines at lunch, trying to keep our Vegemite or fritz-and-sauce (another name for devon and tomato sauce) sandwiches dry, while I stared enviously at the other girls in their steamy cars, heaters on full bore, sipping their soups and munching their not-at-all-damp rolls.

But as each of my horses got old or lame or somehow worried me, I would sell it and buy a new one, a horse that was young and strong, that I could ride and groom and lose myself in until it showed weakness in some way and I passed it on. And I was never happier than when I could lose myself on horseback.

Towards the end of her life, when Katie was old and frail and it was obvious her time was drawing to a close, I pretended that I didn't have a dog. This is classic me. Avoid-the-tough-stuff me.

Katie's eyes clouded, her legs stiffened, and in the last couple of weeks she rarely got out of her kennel. Instead of being a good owner, the kind of person who would put aside her own worry to comfort a dying dog, I looked away. I felt so terrible and afraid when I saw her that I stopped looking. And one day I got home and my brother said she had died and he had buried her in the garden, and I didn't even go to look at the place he had chosen for her.

What hurts the most, what I am most ashamed of, is that I did the same when my beloved grandpa got sick.

When he died.

He took a long time to die, my grandpa. During the time he lived alone, when he had grown frail, I would see Mum brace whenever the phone rang in case it was bad news about him, which more and more frequently it was. When he fell while walking to the shops and needed an ambulance. When he was found wandering the streets because he had forgotten where he lived. And it was worse when there were no calls and my mum and uncle kicked in his door and found him in his collapsed bed, where he had lain for three days and nights in his own filth, not strong enough to get up.

When he moved to the nursing home he often didn't know who we were. He would think I was Mum and call me Susie Q and ask after Mootie, my grandma, his beloved, who had died eighteen years earlier.

He got thinner, frailer; we visited him in hospital and I remember how gaunt he was and that his toenails curled over the edge of the hospital slippers as the nursing home staff had not bothered to cut them for a year and we never knew as he still always wore his brogues and coat with the professor patches, even when he didn't know who he was.

When he went to hospital for the last time I refused to see him. My own discomfort meant I shut my eyes to how sad Mum was, how worried, how she took on the pain of a deathly ill father with the behaviour of a selfish teenage girl and never called me out on it.

On his last day Mum picked me up from a friend's house – as I was still having sleepovers while she worried about her father – and I went with her to the hospital.

Once there I would not get out of the car, my fear of what I would see turning me feral, refusing to look at Mum for fear of what would be in her eyes, snapping at her to get out and go in and leave me be.

She was gone for an hour and I knew, knew, that my grandpa was dead and I had missed it. Worse, I knew that my mum was still thinking of me, putting me first, picking me up from a stupid teenage sleepover when she could have been with her dad in his last moments.

Avoidance is my sordid sanctuary, my ill-disguised safe place, all the while actually making my anxiety cling harder. Making the lives of those I love harder. Worse.

The second time I saw my mum cry was when Grandpa died. My uncle came around to organise the funeral and as I was being shuffled out the door I turned around and saw Mum on the couch, nodding and red eyed, and I felt sick and unstuck. She didn't want to speak at his funeral, too shy to stand in front of the church and talk about her dad, so I read for us, in the chapel of the school he had attended.

And as sad as I was, as much as I missed the grandpa who danced and smelled like tobacco and ham and mustard sandwiches; who showed me how water beads on a geranium leaf; who collected 'bum nuts' from the front-yard tree; who let me build ant cities on his front path (and ant hospitals for the poor sods who didn't survive being handled by a five-year-old); who saved all his coins for me and brought me frilled dresses from London; whose final years were scary and undignified when he forgot who we were even while he remembered to always have Smith's chips in his cupboard and flat Coke in his fridge; worry for whom sent the spiders scurrying in my chest, when the phone rang and the bloated toad in my stomach burped and flobbed and splatted in case it was bad news and he was in pain or sick or missing.

As much as I loved him, I was relieved when it was over.

Other Stories

The next person to write is the blokiest bloke you can imagine. Think strong Aussie accent and scruffy hair and a love of words like 'bloody' and 'oath'. A journo, like me, and used to hearing some of the tough stories.

I had a pretty confronting and traumatic experience as a young kid. In short, my mother twice tried to kill me as a four-year-old after episodes where she had attempted to take her own life as a result of postnatal depression. The result was that it triggered anxiety attacks (pretty regular as a teen but less now) which can be crippling.

The fight-or-flight scenario plays out for me, but I don't think I've ever been in a situation where flight comes into it. If I could bottle and use the adrenaline that comes from a triggered anxiety attack for me, I could outrun Usain Bolt, I reckon. Fortunately, as an adult, it has not been as regular or as intense, 'cause I can recognise when it might happen and can take steps to avoid it. Basically, I get the most full-on rush into my head – adrenaline or blood, whatever it is it feels like molten lava bursting from a volcano. It wouldn't always be obvious to people around me, I'm sure. But step into my space that moment, challenge me, be in my vision, there's every chance you'll cop it.

It is not the result of anger. It is not always a violent response. It is a state for me. That burst of lava lasts just a moment. It will wash over me, blind me, flatten me at times. I'm exhausted after an episode and I usually don't remember or recall what it was that even triggered it. I used to have them often at the sight of my mum. Something about the situation, a sight or a smell, a recollection, can trigger them and usually with her (remembering I was a teen) I would lash out at her. And she'd fight back, don't worry about that.

It got better but didn't completely disappear when I found out, had it confirmed, about the incidents where I was held hostage and threatened. But it is still there.

I had my first attack for a few years only a couple of weeks ago. That rush, my god, it could be a very addictive drug. It also would be a very scary drug. I think it lucky I discovered the truth about the incidents involving Mum at an age where I could better understand she's suffered a mental illness. I was almost seventeen when I was told I wasn't having dreams but recalling the past. It still took a few years before I really accepted that and it wasn't very helpful as my first marriage of eight years broke down. But all sweet now.

My latest incident I can vaguely link to work I'm doing outside in addition to journo stuff with a missing people charity and trying to bust some paedos. My anxiety went up when it looked like I was not going to be able to help with a charity event I'd organised. It wasn't so much frustration or pissed off but that tightness feeling of 'this is going to fall apart, then who's going to help these people', them and another mob I'm involved with are without a voice and they need one, now. The exact thing that triggered the thing/burn/lava, I don't know. I didn't blow up. I would likely have been noticeably different but I was controlled as far as I know. I was in the office. I told a coworker to piss off about five minutes after but that's just because most would tell him to piss off.

Ever had a CT scan in one of those tube/tunnel things and they inject you with the dye? It gives you this big wave of warmth flush through you. Can feel like you've pissed yourself. Anyway, that's the feeling I get through my noggin.

9

Social anxiety

As shy as I have been at times, as much as I have prayed for the carpet to swallow me up rather than having to do another speech on *The Great Gatsby* in front of whispering teenagers and work meetings can still fill me with hot-faced horror, I am mostly an outgoing person.

Actually, I'm probably not the best person at being able to identify exactly what kind of person I am – for a long while I was convinced I was going to be the next Whitney Houston – but I do feel pretty comfortable when it comes to social situations. Sure, I still don't love giving presentations and can sometimes clam up if I am around people I think are smarter or more sophisticated than me; most people, though, will feel some kind of discomfort in certain social situations: when they walk into the party alone, starting a new job, going on a first date. Today, I could generally give zero shits whether people like me or not.

So I'm lucky, because I think there is a particularly acute kind of agony that must come with social anxiety. Being swamped by waves freaks me out but I don't have to think about that (too much) when I am just going down the shops for a pasty. I am paranoid about germs, no question, but unless someone coughs on me or vomits in my general vicinity then I can mostly pretend I am normal.

However, fearing social situations because you think you will be found to be stupid or ridiculous or look the fool must be the constant rub, because unless you have the means to lock yourself away in a cave somewhere, most days you will have to interact with someone.

There are lots of problematic ways people choose to deal with their social anxiety, and avoidance rears its ugly head in most.

My mother, who will chat away at home even if no one is paying much attention, will only say the bare minimum when out in public. I've asked her why plenty of times over the years as I could never work out why my friends' mums were out all the time with their friends whereas my mum had just one good friend, Lori, who would come over for coffee and smoke countless cigarettes at the kitchen table while Mum, who has never smoked in her life, would put out an ashtray and try very hard not to cough.

Lori and Mum had met sharing a hospital room after giving birth to their first babies. Mum had me at twenty-seven – after a labour that lasted more than a day, she pushed me out without drugs or making a sound. Lori's son Paul was born three days earlier and Lori was already set up in bed when Mum was wheeled in to take the bed next to her.

Their friendship never made a whole lot of sense to me – do adult relationships ever make sense to kids? – but even as a small thing I could see their differences.

The way Lori did most of the talking and Mum nodded and smiled. I remember them sitting around the table one wintry day, smoke curling thickly in the air like the room was some kind of backstreet gambling den, when Lori – whose marriage had ended – huffed and said, very loudly, 'Oh GOD, don't you ever just want to get laid?' I must have been at least twelve as I knew what she meant, at least in the most abstract sense, and I glanced at Mum and saw her mumble something quietly as Lori took another drag on her ciggie.

But aside from Lori, Mum and Dad didn't have any friends, not that I ever saw.

Of course, because she is my mum I never thought to ask her about it, to find out why she is who she is, until now. She is just Mum, like all mums. But she is the first to admit that she finds social interaction very hard, and can pinpoint the moment she thinks it all began.

At just two (what is it with the age two? Someone should really do something scientificky on that) Mum had gone along with her mum on a social visit.

She remembers it as clearly as I remember the drowning hole and sent me an email when I asked her to describe where she thinks her social phobia started and why it has lingered so long, because sometimes these things are easier to express through your fingers than lips.

The big fat ginger cat stared at me from the front verandah of my mother's friend's house. I had been taken for a visit when we first moved down from the country. I was two years old; the ginger cat was all I could see. It stared at me with huge yellow eyes, I just wanted to watch.

'What's your name?' asked my mother's friend. I didn't answer, if I moved or spoke the cat might run away.

After a few moments my mother spoke, 'Susan doesn't talk, she's shy'. From then on I had the perfect excuse – clearly 'shy' meant not talking.

At ten, the nuns at my convent school chose me to be spokesperson for the school at a combined schools concert. I only had about four lines to say and had rehearsed them so often that I knew them faultlessly. When the curtains opened, there I was, standing at the microphone, blinking through the lights at all the eyes focused on me. I couldn't remember any of the lines; my memory was a complete blank. Several awkward minutes later, one of the nuns came to the rescue and ushered me off stage. I was mortified.

My two brothers were a lot older than me and incredibly high achievers at school. Both won awards including topping the state in school exams. I knew I could never live up to their standards and this had an impact on my self-confidence and self-esteem. When my marks suffered at high school because I couldn't see any point in trying, my well-meaning father would say, 'It's okay, girls don't need to have a career'. This reinforced my opinion that I was really quite unimportant and had nothing of any importance to contribute.

When it came to noticing boys for the first time, I tried to make myself as invisible as possible. I could see them wanting to approach me but I was so scared that they would talk to me and realise that I had nothing interesting to say.

I hate being the centre of attention and this means that in group situations I don't talk much. This has resulted in me being called a snob; people tend to take my silence personally. This also affected my work; chairing meetings was hell, I wouldn't make eye contact and loathed every minute.

Working as a social worker at a health centre, I interviewed several residents from a retirement village about their memories. These stories were then printed out for them in a book. The senior social worker was so impressed that she wanted me to exhibit the book at a regional meeting of social workers. I couldn't do it, it would mean being the centre of attention and that was unbearable.

I felt a complete shit when I read what Mum wrote.

For years, all my life, with sympathy and love she has tried to help me manage my anxiety, and for years I wanted her to get some friends or an amazingly impressive job so she would be like the other mums I knew. What Mum wrote also showed that the way we think about ourselves is so often different to how others perceive us. And why social anxiety doesn't bear up to critical thinking, as we can never be sure of how others see us.

When I was pulling yet another sickie from school I would often go along with Mum to her work to avoid the boredom at home. For a while she worked at a shelter for young single mothers. She was in charge of the day care centre where the mums would leave their kids while they went to school classes or outings with the nuns who ran the place. I do not like small kids, for the most part, as they are messy and grabby and often have snot leaking out of their noses, and they smell vaguely (on a good day) like poo. So I would watch from a safe vantage point, nose buried in a book but eyes peeking over the top, while Mum worked. To me she seemed in control, confident, calm, wise. Nothing seemed to faze her. Throw a screaming kid at her – there were many, and sometimes they even had tattoos already – and she would beatifically soothe them with a quiet song or a jiggle on her knee.

The young mothers loved her and after she quit many took the bus up to our house to visit her. I think she made them feel respected and safe, often for the first time in their lives.

Social anxiety is one of the most common anxiety disorders; Mum is most definitely not alone. One of the things you can do if you have it and would much rather you didn't is to observe yourself as it happens. To be able to learn to manage social anxiety you first need to understand it. If you can identify the types of social situations that freak you out and the way that anxiety manifests – maybe blushing or sweating or something else – it will be easier to recognise when it happens and learn how to manage it. You might even want to write it down, note the situation and the symptoms because it can often be hard to remember the particulars of an episode once the fear has passed. The brain doesn't particularly want to hold on to that information.

Once you recognise your symptoms, there are a couple of things you can do to lessen them. Calm breathing is helpful no matter what kind of anxiety you have. Slow breathing activates the parasympathetic nervous system (sometimes called the 'rest and digest' system), which slows the heart rate. Breathing quickly – which many of us do when we are anxious – can lead to some of the symptoms that make you feel so crap. Things like light-headedness, which can make you even more anxious because you feel like you might keel over in front of all the people stressing you out in the first place.

Yogis have a fantastic mode of breathing – pranayama – which I have found powerfully effective when other modes of slow breathing have felt impossible. When I am freaking out and feel like I can't catch my breath, other modes of slow breathing still leave me feeling like I can't fill my lungs.

The pranayama technique I use involves inhaling through your nose and then exhaling through your open mouth, making a drawn-out *ha* sound from the back of your throat. Once you've worked out that you have the right action, you close your mouth and focus on breathing in and out through your nose while dragging the breath across the back of the throat where it will, hopefully, make a soft hissing sound. The practice is known as *ujjayi pranayama* and you can see good examples of it online if my explanation is confusing.

I find it impossible to overbreathe when I practise pranayama and I am no yogi. When I am doing it right I can feel the rest of my body unclench and still, the rigidity of anxiety releasing.

Muscle relaxation is another thing you might find helpful. It's the kind of thing you may have done in the classroom as a kid when the teacher made you all lie down because she needed a second to not be answering millions of questions like, 'Miss, can a dog and a cat have sex?' All you need to do is go around your body mentally, tensing and relaxing muscles. If you'd like to have someone else guide you through something similar, look for practices called *yoga nidra*.

●

You probably wouldn't be anxious in social situations if you didn't have negative thoughts swirling around your head telling you that 'no one will like me', or 'everyone thinks I'm boring', or 'I'll do something stupid and people will laugh'. It's important to start thinking about your thoughts as just that – thoughts – and not as facts or certainties. Realistic thinking is the goal but it's not easy (god, if it was I wouldn't be writing this book).

By learning to challenge your thoughts – by seeing them as guesses rather than unshakeable realities – you can challenge them with evidence. It's also important to realise that everyone says dumb stuff sometimes, and not everyone will like you, and this is fine and normal.

Like all anxiety, the most important bit is to face your fear. It definitely makes you feel better in the short term to just not go to that party you are dreading, but you're not learning that what you fear is unlikely to happen or isn't as bad as you think it will be – plus think of all the free food and booze you are missing (and you'll see friends, *blah blah*).

Start with something you don't find too scary – maybe having a conversation with the person who makes your coffee in the morning or saying g'day to the person next to you in the lift – and work your way up to the really terrifying stuff: the work presentation, going to a function alone. If you find yourself getting pissed to deal with social events, try to have one drink instead of a gazillion, as booze is just one of the more subtle methods of avoidance.

Don't stop there! Once you've conquered the known, get out there and try the unknown. Join that belly-dancing class you've been thinking about, go speed dating – cripes, join a nudist colony if that takes your fancy. And when things get tough and you find yourself reaching for a bottle of tequila and cancelling all functions for the foreseeable future, remember that anxiety sucks and rears its ugly head when times are tough. Start at the beginning again, start testing the thoughts, and you'll get back on track.

Don't just take my word for it, though: go and see someone if anxiety is overwhelming your life. You never have to challenge it alone.

Other Stories

I met E when I joined a mothers' group after my first son was born. She is bright and bold with a big laugh; someone who can laugh at the dodgy blokes who contact her on online dating sites but is willing to give the shy ones a go.

She has anxiety.

My anxiety started, I think, around primary school age. The first thing I really remember was when I suddenly became scared that I would need to go to the toilet when out in public, that I wouldn't be able to hold on and would wet my pants. That never happened but what it did result in was that no matter what sort of outing I was on, I would always need to go to the toilet (I think just to make sure there was one). So at the movies, plays for school, anything like that where we were somewhere enclosed, I would need to go to the toilet. That's pretty tame, really.

Then I became afraid of vomiting in public. I was worried that at any time, in a crowded public place, I might suddenly vomit. This started in my teenage years and I am still a bit afraid of it today. This was when I started sitting at the edge. I would sit at the edge of the cinema, any sort of theatre, on the bus, all so I could make a speedy exit if I needed to vomit. In public I always knew where the bins were. I never vomited.

At age seventeen I got stuck for about one minute in a lift with my boyfriend in his dad's office building. I thought we were never going to get out and that I was going to die. That brought on a fear of lifts that lasted about ten years. I worked at David Jones at the time, on the sixth floor, and got very fit climbing the stairs every time I went to work. I worked there for four years and probably only went in the lift once or twice. I still have dreams of getting stuck in lifts or people dying in lifts. I make sure I go to the toilet before I go in the lift just in case something happens. I used to have to check out events before I went to them – if there was a lift involved I had to always make sure I could have access to stairs.

I have always been anxious going out in public. I used to rehearse what I would say to the bus driver when I bought my ticket to go to uni, every day. I was worried everyone on the bus was looking at me and was paranoid of embarrassing myself. To this day when I walk down the street I think people are watching me. If I have to go somewhere new, like a new restaurant or café, I will worry for days and try to take someone with me so I don't have to go alone.

I can't eat in front of new or potential partners, so virtually starve myself. I have told myself this is normal but apparently it's not.

In 2007 when I travelled to Nepal alone, I spent months in my hotel room as I was too scared to go out on my own despite it being my third trip there and knowing my way around really well. I was scared of people staring at me.

I take Lexapro daily or I can't function and the daily anxiety escalates and the whole world just becomes too difficult.

Medication won't be the solution for everyone – and some people don't want it to work for them, thinking drugs provide an inauthentic peace – but E has found something that helps her get through each day. Sometimes that's enough.

I am the glass half empty. The doom and gloom. The sad sack. If I had to draw my essence I would use lots of red and black texta with some squiggly yellow bits

10

Positive negativity

Pessimists get a bad rap.

We live in an age where positivity and optimism are lauded, where slogans like 'If You Can Dream It, You Can Achieve It' and 'Manifest Your Own Reality' are printed on T-shirts and regurgitated in corporate workshops; 'Magic Happens' is slapped on the back of the four-wheel drive full of screaming kids, and 'Everything Happens for a Reason' is shared with a smile and a patted hand at your nan's funeral.

Self-help gurus crow that all that stands between you and success – happiness! – is the right mindset, a determination to believe the positive and embody it, and an openness to receive all of the wonderful and fulfilling things the universe has in store for you if only you will let them in.

I really want to believe this stuff. How wonderful it would be if the universe really did have my ideal existence already mapped out for me, that if I think 'right' then it will manifest. That if I focus my mind on how excellent my day will be, how smoothly everything will go, how seamlessly I will deal with hurdles, everything will be, in fact, awesome.

Sadly, I am the glass half empty. The doom and gloom. The sad sack. If I had to draw my essence I would use lots of red and black texta with some squiggly yellow bits on the outside being consumed by maniacal brown globs.

But I would very much like to be something else.

At various points in my life (and especially in my late teens and early twenties) I have been desperate to be the happy optimist, the type who laughs in the face of life's inconsistencies and travesties and gross diseases. The type who ends each day knowing everything is exactly as it should be, that the days to come will unfold as they should.

I have bought *dozens* of self-help books over the years, the ones that promise happiness if I repeat this mantra, watch the sunrise every morning, remember to be grateful.

I tried to appreciate *The Celestine Prophecy* when everyone started to wet their pants about it in the early 1990s. Friends would walk around with it tucked under an arm, beatific expressions on their faces; some said it changed their lives and 'paid it forward' with a trite dedication scrawled inside the cover accompanied by lots of *xxxx*s and *oooo*s.

I read it and, although I tried to love it, all I felt was annoyed. I found a copy of it on a shelf when I first moved in with my now-husband. He had scrawled a dedication on the inside cover, a heartfelt pledge to an ex that he 'hoped it would speak to her heart as much as it spoke to his'. Desperately wresting it from my hand as I held it, mouth agape, he tore the inscription from the binding and stuffed it into his mouth, chewing it into a wet pulp. It was a make-or-break night. Later that evening I also found some of those velcro sandals German travellers like to wear and it was almost the death of us.

I tried, oh how I tried, to be that girl: the positive one, the happy one, the light one, the one who wouldn't shriek and point, and post about the travel sandals on Facebook. But it's not the best fun, or most productive endeavour, to rail so frantically against who you intrinsically are.

When I was eighteen I tried to pretend to be a surfie for a couple of months. I can't swim and I hate waves but I plugged away regardless. Mum and Dad gave me a boogie board for Christmas – not a real one but a fluoro-pink foam one from Kmart, although I didn't know the difference – and I carried it on 'surf trips' down south in the middle of winter. Freezing cold, I watched friends pull on their wetsuits with gritted teeth before they trotted, blue and goose-fleshed, down to the water. I waited in the car and watched them blob about on the piddling waves, eyes peeled for fins. Truthfully I was never really that committed – my fear of drowning being more intense than my fear of social isolation – but we stopped for the good pies on the way home.

Then I tried being a metal-music fan. I was going out with a boy who shared a house with a very glamorous blond girl who wore a bright slash of red lipstick at all times and blowdried her hair aggressively until it stood up in a wave above her forehead. Their lounge was furnished with milk crates and a bong, and when she walked into the room he would gaze moonily at her while I sat in my wrong jeans and silk neck-scarf (my Proper Lady phase) and glowered.

Soon I was wearing a black-and-white flannie, faux-listening to Pantera, and fake-smoking bummed cigarettes outside smelly venues in dark alleys. On Tuesday nights we sat around the milk crate, under a fugue of smoke, listening as one maudlin mane after another whinged about the death of real music. Then they would all play on their PlayStation while I slunk off to read.

When I was nineteen I tried to buy a Byron Bay–based tofu-hotdog stand. I spent New Year's Eve at Woodford Folk Festival in the semi-rainforest and gambolled awkwardly in front of folk bands, self-consciously performing a wavy arm-dance in a paddock. I weed into a cup inside my tent rather than brave the portaloos which percolated in the sun like hellish coffee machines. I bought tarot cards and spoke to a psychic who said I should do my tax. I scoured markets for sarongs and wore an anklet. I bought Louise Hay's books and spoke to my spleen and went to a homeopath. I smelled of nag champa incense and listened earnestly as someone called Oracle droned in my face about psychic healing.

Then I jumped in a car with two friends and we headed for the Byron Bay Blues Festival. As it was raining torrentially, my friends cast off their shoes with abandon and leapt gleefully about in the mud. I tried, I really did. But after half an hour I trotted back to the car and read my book with the heater on, giving the sporadic finger to drunks who approached our SA-plated car looking for weed.

Nothing fit.

But there is a subgroup, subversive, that believes thinking negatively isn't necessarily a terrible thing if it can be harnessed in the right way. Like some intractable pony that stomps all over your feet while the others trot around obligingly in perfect circles, pessimism will kick you in the guts until you work out how to make it work for you.

Julie Norem, professor of psychology at Massachusetts' Wellesley College, has been extolling the virtues of negative thinking for decades.

Author of *The Positive Power of Negative Thinking*, Norem writes about 'defensive pessimism', which, essentially, is a strategy anxious people sometimes use to help manage their anxiety by setting low expectations and then mentally rehearsing (in concrete, specific detail) all the things that might go wrong.[1]

I had found my people.

Except bog-standard catastrophising – the type I am expert in – is not enough. The important bit is to focus on the concrete detail of what could go wrong, because it helps anxious people shift their attention away from how they are feeling towards their goals. So when they think in detail about what might go wrong, they also identify ways to prevent those catastrophes and the detail helps them identify specific actions that are not overwhelming but get them working toward their goals.

It is the concrete detail that separates positive pessimism from catastrophising.

'One of the problems with anxiety is that ignoring it rarely works, and people often avoid anxiety-producing situations (which can keep them out of a lot of important situations), or they feel immobilized [sic] and overwhelmed,' Norem wrote when I emailed her some appropriately anxious questions about her theory.

'Thus a strategy that focuses on specifics and helps people move toward action can be very effective. For example, if I'm anxious about a presentation I have to give at work, I might play through what could go wrong: the Powerpoint presentation won't work because the projector bulb will burn out or, even if it does work, the slides won't be clear, and the manager from accounting always asks hard budget questions, and I'm klutzy so I might trip on my way to the head of the table et cetera et cetera. As I identify each of these specific problems it also becomes easier to prevent or deal with them. I can show up early to the meeting room to double-check the equipment and corral a colleague to go through the slides looking for ways to make them clearer. I can meet with someone from accounting to get a grip on the numbers before the presentation, and have that person come up with every question they possibly can. I can make sure I'm wearing sensible shoes so I'm less likely to stumble, and clear the path between my chair and the podium before everyone arrives.

'It can sound OCD or just a little ridiculous but taking the first action is often the hardest part for anxious people, so a strategy that helps them do that is powerful.'

In the same situation the catastrophiser might start with the fairly contained negative thought but, within moments, is imagining their worst nightmare: 'I'm worried my talk won't go well, then I'll lose my job, and then I won't be able to pay rent and I'll end up on the street, pimping out my body before ending up dead in an alley.'[2]

After researching defensive pessimism for thirty years, Norem has been able to refine and extend her theory.

Early on, it was assumed that people using more optimistic strategies spent significant time and effort thinking about how well everything would go when they faced a performance situation. Think about all of the wellness experts directing you to visualise the things you want and to think positively. Research showed, however, that optimists tend *not* to think about how things will unfold before the fact. Instead, they distract themselves from thoughts about upcoming performances or potentially anxiety-producing situations.

In all of Norem's research, anxious people who use defensive pessimism do better (are happier, more satisfied, perform better) than anxious people who do not use defensive pessimism.

In most of her studies, defensive pessimists perform as well as more optimistic, non-anxious individuals, and there are some contexts where they perform *better*. The costs and benefits vary by person, situation and cultural context (there are several studies from Japan and China that find defensive pessimists performing better than optimists, but that may be the case because those cultural contexts place less emphasis on positive self-presentation and more emphasis on modesty and circumspection).[3]

Interestingly (and frustratingly for those who thought they might have found their anxiety cure), experiencing positive outcomes by following defensive pessimism strategies – finding the concrete details – doesn't seem to make an anxious person less likely to fret about outcomes. And there are probably a few reasons why.

First, people probably do become less anxious about specific outcomes that they worried about a lot in the past, but as they experience more success they tend to set higher goals. As they think about these higher goals they imagine new things that might stuff them up, even while acknowledging that past worries are no longer relevant.

Second, when people use defensive pessimism they tend to believe that it is the key to their success ('As it probably is', adds Norem), so they become reluctant to give it up for fear they'll fail without it.

Third, people who are prone to anxiety are unlikely to stop feeling anxious generally due to other root causes (like genetic and environmental influences) but by using defensive pessimism their *anxiety about being anxious* is likely to decrease.

This is good news for anxious people, who can be tipped into anxiety because they are worried about their anxiety affecting their performance in certain situations.

And there are limitations to defensive pessimism.

'It takes effort and thus can be tiring,' Norem says. 'Ideally people use it in important situations, not for everyday things like driving to the grocery store (although if one is anxious about going to the grocery store/driving it's probably better to use an effortful strategy and actually get to the grocery store and back than to fret and stew and exhaust yourself while never making the trip).'

Plus there is, of course, the culturally anarchic fallout of being a pessimist in an optimist's world.

'Especially where optimism, positive thinking, and confident self-presentation are highly valued, defensive pessimism can bring others down, make others doubt your abilities, and/or make others feel as if they should cheer you up. The social consequences can be significant,' Norem writes. 'I frequently remind defensive pessimists that others may not respond well to their strategy (especially if you are pointing out all the things that could go wrong in someone else's plan – rarely appreciated), that it can be helpful to explain their strategy to others so they're not branded as "the negative one". I also emphasize [sic] that they don't need to do it "out loud" in front of other people, it works just as well when done inside one's head.'

Moreover, what if the source of your anxiety is not the important presentation, or the uncomfortable first date, or the final exam, but something less tangible? Can defensive pessimism work for the intractable hypochondriac, say? Yes, if you are willing to set some goals and risk feeling uncomfortable.

'I think the key in this domain is to start with setting goals and then to apply defensive pessimism to those goals,' Norem says.

'So, for example, someone who is anxious about health issues may consult medical personnel about their health history and current status and get a list of their most salient health risks, thus focussing their anxiety on specific issues, rather than automatically worrying about every possible disease out there.

'Rather than telling a worried person not to worry . . . I would try to focus them on the most likely probability and then apply defensive pessimism to planning ways to avoid that. Again, action/doing something is better than stewing, so even if they're spending disproportionate effort on a specific risk, they are still being active, rather than panicking and catastrophising.'

I don't know what's wrong with me that I find it so hard to actually do something instead of just stewing (I mean, I know *what's* wrong with me, but I don't know *why*). Maybe laziness, maybe still the fear that if I try something I will have proof that I can't do it.

If I don't try then I can hold on to the belief that if I *did*, I *could*.

It still can feel safer to live in the untested belief, the future unfounded, than risk failure. At night, in the safety of my warm bed, there is a certain comfort to be found in dreaming of how wonderful my future will be, how successful and healthy and safe. While the idea that this could become real – that I could really live that life – is sweet, the fear of being found wanting, of not being good enough to get there, to have it wrenched away, is the psychological door slammed shut. The reason why the unrealised fantasy might always be better than the reality denied.

Within moments, actual seconds,
I am convinced they are dying, then
I am dying, we are all dying, and
it is hopeless.

11

Health anxiety and emetophobia

When I lived in Queensland in my late twenties, I was convinced I had cancer in my abdomen.

I can't remember what set this off but I do remember prodding at my tummy to work out if it was sore compared with how it felt the day before; eventually, whether it was an overactive imagination or just all that prodding, I did have a pain that hovered vaguely under my navel in a niggly-achey way.

After obsessing for weeks, imagining how terrible it would be to die before I turned thirty, how tragic, such potential unfulfilled, until I scared myself thoroughly enough – and annoyed my now-husband enough with my constant what-iffing – that I was convinced to make an appointment with a doctor. I shared my fears – that I had a tumour of unknown origin – and after some general poking she said she would send me for a scan, even though she couldn't feel anything odd.

I freaked, thinking that being sent for more testing meant that the doctor believed there could be something seriously wrong with me and squirmed about for days in anticipation of my appointment.

When I finally got there, sitting on the table with my pants off while waiting for the ultrasound technician, I snuck a look at the referral.

The doctor had written, in what looked to me like sarcastic inverted commas, 'Patient is convinced she has a tumour'. I was suddenly embarrassed: I saw myself as I imagined the doctor saw me, as some weird malingerer who visited doctors for perverted kicks.

While the tech did the scan I made jokes – 'Ha ha, just thought I would come and see you as I love internal scans, ha ha, I don't really think I have a tumour, oh ha ha haaaa' – while he looked, nonplussed, at the screen.

There was, of course, no tumour but I did score a wonderful internal ultrasound out of the experience. You haven't really lived until a man old enough to be your grandfather has stuck an electronic ultrasound wand wearing a condom up your whatsit.

•

History puts hypochondriacs like me in great company – Charles Darwin, Andy Warhol, Howard Hughes, Edgar

Allen Poe, Charlotte Brontë and Florence Nightingale were all hypochondriacs to varying degrees – but it's still a pretty embarrassing issue to have, especially when it affects you to such a disabling extent that you can't even sit in a theatre for fear the person next to you will chunder everywhere and infect you with some intractable disease.

Hypochondriasis – or health anxiety, as it is now more commonly known – is an overwhelming fear that you have a serious illness even though health professionals can't find anything wrong with you. People with hypochondriasis misinterpret normal sensations as evidence that there is something seriously wrong with their bodies.

Most people will worry about their health from time to time – when they find a weird lump or have a cough they can't shake – but the health phobic worries incessantly and out of all proportion to the realistic likelihood that they are actually at risk. Plus it's just really unfun.

When my kids are sick I will comfort them and wipe their clammy brows but I will also be consumed by panic, more so than the average worried parent. I will scan through my limited but gory mental inventory of all the things that could possibly fit their symptoms and then fixate on the most disastrous. Within moments, actual seconds, I am convinced they are dying, then I am dying, we are all dying, and it is hopeless.

I almost died just recently.

Against my better judgement I sat next to a person-of-questionable-hygiene on the bus and within days my face was leaking and my throat ached and I was convinced I had swine flu and was not long for this world.

The one thing guaranteed to push me over the slippery edge of anxiety into full-blown panic is sickness, a tendency not helped by an obsession with medical books and the television show *Embarrassing Bodies*, which I still don't understand – is it some kind of trick? Why would someone be too embarrassed to show their GP their prolapsed vagina or discuss with them their six-year genital itch but be quite happy for the whole world, and potentially all their ex-boyfriends, ex-boyfriends' new partners, their boss and their dad to see?

I think I am doing quite well on the anxiety front and then I get a headache and moments later I am searching the internet for information on bubonic plague. In the course of the last year I was convinced I had, in no particular order and to name but a few: diabetes, ovarian and stomach cancer, pneumonia, meningitis, and early-onset dementia.

My fear of falling deathly ill is so strong, so overwhelming, that it has informed and controlled much of my life.

I've thought long and hard about why a fear of sickness has been so pervasive, has lasted when other phobias and anxieties have faded and disappeared. The best I can come up with is that sickness, to me, is the perfect storm of inevitability and unpredictability. We all get sick, all of us – even if I locked myself in a room away from everyone I might still succumb to some opportunistic bacteria or dodgy sandwich. Might still be struck down by some genetic disease or rogue cells multiplying out of control.

So there is the knowledge that I am going to get sick, but I don't know when, and I can't guarantee how badly. I can wash my hands and take vitamins and eat well and exercise, try to exert some measure of control, but I will still, at some point, get sick.

And then, if I knew a cold was just a cold, it wouldn't scare me. If I knew a fever was just part of a virus and would be gone by tomorrow with no complications, I could relax. But it is the unknowable, uncontrollable, unpredictable, inevitable nature of sickness that terrifies me.

My time as a health reporter has in no way made me feel better about sickness. I have interviewed people who lost their children unexpectedly when they succumbed to routine childhood illnesses. I've interviewed terribly sad people waiting desperately for a cure; people who were perfectly fine one day and disabled the next. The fragility of life is very obvious to me. I can't work out why everyone isn't deathly afraid.

The more grotesque an illness, the messier, the more afraid of it I will be.

Leprosy, which, in my mind, covered a person in oozing sores, leaving them with blackened rotting stumps, tortured me for years.

Gastro – I shudder even typing the word – is awful. It used to be that I was just scared that it would happen to me, that I would be fine one minute and vomiting explosively somewhere public the next. Today I worry about my kids getting it from the other kids at school, as they will be fine one minute and spewing through the car or their beds the next.

Emetophobia (fear of vomiting) and disgust sensitivity are tied together. Studies show that those who are more sensitive to feelings of disgust are more likely to fear vomiting.[1] One study showed that people with vomit phobia are much better at recalling episodes where other people vomited before their phobia began than a control group.[2]

In his excellent book *My Age of Anxiety*, Scott Stossel describes going through exposure therapy in an attempt to get rid of his extreme fear of vomiting. Although he has gone more than thirty-five years without throwing up, he fears it incessantly. Oh, how I know how he feels.

After several attempts to desensitise Stossel to vomiting – which were unsuccessful because there was no real inherent risk of Stossel vomiting – his therapist thought there was only one way to accomplish it: Stossel had to vom.

After making and then cancelling multiple vomit appointments, Stossel was, at last, dosed liberally with ipecac and then his therapist and a nurse waited for the vomit to erupt, to show Stossel that he didn't die and all was fine and there was nothing to fear. They waited. And they waited. He heaved, sure – heaved and heaved and lay on the tiled floor between bouts of more heaving covered in a cold sweat. But he didn't vomit. At the end of the session, which eventually caused his therapist to spew because she was so nauseated by his constant retching, Stossel was even more phobic about vomiting.[3]

My own efforts at avoiding vomiting have also been Herculean. Growing up, as other family members toppled one by one to gastro, I would swallow the sick feeling crawling up my throat and simply forbid myself from vomiting. The idea of vomiting was so repellent, so disastrous, that it simply could not be countenanced. No vomit for me.

But there is something to be said for exposure therapy, even if exposure comes about by less deliberate means. I am no longer scared of vomiting – in fact, I would go so far as to say I even welcome a vom if I am feeling truly ill – and it is all thanks to my eldest son. Morning sickness cured me of my fear of vomiting. So constant was my feeling of sickness during early pregnancy, so vile was the spew, so exhausted was I generally, that I think I just didn't have the energy to devote to spew-panic *and* standing up.

Yet health phobia remains. To me, a rash is always meningococcal, a cough is pneumonia, an ache is cancer, listlessness is a step away from one of the strange viruses that kill healthy children.

But then a large part of my fear is also knee-jerk in nature. I don't know why my child coughing in the night makes my heart seize. I don't know why I was so scared of vomit. No one loves it – it is messy and foul – but I *feared* it. People with health anxiety are inhabited by fear. And the anticipatory fear is always worse than the reality.

People with health anxiety tend to be more aware of their bodily sensations and more likely to interpret them the wrong way, and this is absolutely true of my own brain and the way it will choose to see a rumbly tummy as ovarian cancer instead of a reaction to having Twisties for breakfast. My brain is also very good at fixating on my body even when everything feels fine. It conducts whole-body scans multiple times a day, just to see if something feels different or strange or numb or anything other than 'normal'.

No one knows for sure what causes health anxiety but there are certain things that may put a person at risk, including major life stress, a history of child abuse, a family history of health anxiety, or having another mental disorder like depression, general anxiety or OCD.

One of the theories around the development of health anxiety posits that it is often found in those who suffered a serious illness as a child, or who were exposed to someone close to them suffering.

The worst sicknesses I had as a kid were bronchitis and a mild case of chicken pox. In fact (touch wood), the people I am surrounded by seem to enjoy rudely good health. There is no chronic disease, no asthma, diabetes, epilepsy. I must be one of the only people to not have a close relative with cancer. But, because my brain is superstitious, even writing this feels like a grave mistake, as if I am daring the universe to undo my good luck, letting it know that it missed one, that it is my turn to suffer.

I want desperately to touch wood. Stupid.

But I do remember Mum going away for a couple of weeks; I was so young that the memories only come in flashes. Holding Dad's hand and walking through sliding doors into the bright beyond. Nanna coming to our house to make dinner and change Ben's pooey nappies. Adults talking in quiet voices over my head.

I only know why she was gone because of what I have learned since.

At a school reunion Mum sat by the pool, keeping an eye on the children playing as her old school friends talked and laughed nearby. Surrounded by splashing, there was one quiet space between the children, and a little girl floated face down, legs and fingers trailing. Mum jumped into the pool and hauled the child to the edge. While others rushed to pull her out, Mum felt a tearing in her belly, like a hole had been created.

A week later, bleeding, Mum went to the doctor and was soon in surgery, where they found a large mass on her ovary. When she woke they told her she had cancer and only weeks to live.

I was three and the doctors wouldn't let us visit Mum for ten days, surely a lifetime for a toddler who was used to her mum always being there.

Just like a clichéd midday movie, though, the doctors were mistaken and it wasn't cancer – just a huge, but ultimately harmless, fibroid. Mum was soon home, albeit needing help because of the surgery, and it was forgotten.

Did I hear someone say that Mum had cancer? Or did the fear of those around me, when they thought Mum was dying, somehow infect me too? There's no way to know now, and it's possible I would be a hopeless hypochondriac anyway, just like my grandma.

However, maybe there is something there, in the disappearance of someone dearer to me than myself, someone who seemed perfectly okay one minute and was then spoken about in whispers over the head of a small child who didn't understand the words but who knew fear.

There are two ways people with health anxiety tackle their fear and, again, it is through avoidance or control.

Controllers are the ones at the doctor's surgery every week; they are the ones Googling symptoms, visiting emergency departments, the reassurance seekers.

Then there are the avoiders, like me. No matter what sickness I think I have, the thought of it being confirmed is worse. As terrible as I feel when I am fixating and obsessing, the chance my imagined malaise could be real is worse and overwhelms the possibility that relief could be found, however briefly, by being given the all-clear. The few times I have gone to the doctor with one of my mystery ailments I have been given the all-clear and the relief is the most enormous high, like a cool stream running through my chest. And it lasts for a while – a couple of weeks, months – until my body does something else strange and I am sucked back down again.

False assumptions are a big part of health anxiety – that bodily changes are always a sign something is not right, that if I don't worry about my health something awful will happen, that if a doctor sends me for a test it is because they think there is something terribly wrong with me.

One of the reasons anxiety is so hard to get rid of is because, for all intents and purposes and to the confused anxious mind, it is keeping you alive and safe.

I'm scared of getting badly sick and dying, ditto for the kids, so I am anxious and hypervigilant and we are all still alive, ergo, my anxiety is keeping us safe. I am afraid to relax that perceived control for even a moment, because if it is true – if it is this keeping us safe – and I relax and someone dies, there is no changing my mind, no taking it back.

People with health anxiety (also known as illness anxiety disorder) strongly believe they have a serious or life-threatening illness despite having no, or only mild symptoms. If they are able to get to the doctor and discover they are fine, they may feel reassured for a while, only for the anxiety to come back, or may think the doctor is wrong and then their obsessive worry continues.

Sometimes health anxiety occurs in people who are physically sick but who think they are much sicker than they really are. It's about the psychological reaction, not the presence or absence of illness.

There are some great online resources to start to deal with health anxiety. For me, while many of the techniques were familiar as I'd done CBT with psychs, just seeing some of my beliefs in black and white lessened their power.

Ever since I first heard of it, meningococcal has been one of my recurring health obsessions, especially in regard to my kids. Part of this is because I have written several stories about people with it and this makes it seem far more common to me than it actually is. Meningococcal takes hold quickly and can resemble everyday illnesses like gastro or flu to start with, before quickly revealing itself as more serious. And it can be fatal or wreak enormous physical destruction. I find it terrifying but, because not many others I shared my fear with had even heard of it, I started to believe that there was a reason I feared this illness in particular, that perhaps the universe or some higher power was making me aware because it was going to affect someone I loved and I was being given all the knowledge I needed to avert catastrophe, and if I didn't act on it, it would be all my fault when that person – one of my kids – died.

So, when reading Perth's Centre for Clinical Interventions' (CCI) Helping Health Anxiety information online, it was enormously helpful, almost transformative for that particular fear, to see it explicitly mentioned. Maybe my fear didn't mean anything after all; maybe none of it means anything; all the fears are random and meaningless.

Dr Lisa Saulsman, senior clinical psychologist at CCI, describes health anxiety as an all-consuming worry, the kind that will occupy the mind of the person suffering it much of the time.

While avoidance is my particularly crappy coping strategy of choice, Dr Saulsman says 'checking' is a more typical response. 'People become excessively preoccupied with trying to "solve" the perceived health problem via seeking lots of reassurance from doctors, medical tests, family, friends, searching the internet to self-diagnose, checking their bodies for signs of illness, and so on,' she wrote in an email.[4]

'When we are mentally and behaviourally preoccupied with our health in this manner, it causes us significant distress and starts to detract from us being able to live the life we want, then "normal" health anxiety has moved into the realms of being a psychological problem that needs to be addressed.'

Health anxiety is not rare. While surveys have shown that anxiety disorders are the most common mental health condition in Australia, with twenty-five per cent of the adult population experiencing an anxiety disorder during their lifetime, health anxiety has not been specifically surveyed.[5]

But Dr Saulsman says, anecdotally, CCI receives many clients referred with health anxiety as either their primary problem or one of a range of difficulties. 'I am not sure there is a typical sufferer, but there will tend to be commonalities in what led to the development of the problem.'

'We know that biologically we can have a genetic vulnerability to developing an anxiety disorder, but what particular anxiety disorder manifests tends to be shaped by people's life experiences. The sorts of life experiences that tend to contribute to the development of health anxiety generally centre on negative experiences regarding their own or others' health. These experiences can then lead to the development of broader beliefs that health – either generally speaking or their own health specifically – is a vulnerable or fragile thing . . . which sets the scene for developing health anxiety, as any sensation or symptom will then be considered to be a sign of ill health.'

Most commonly, she writes, people with health anxiety have witnessed others with a serious illness that was painful or led to death, personally experienced a significant medical problem, observed a family member with health anxiety constantly worrying about health, or have been exposed via the media or internet to stories of rare, fatal, incurable diseases which increases the sense that they are likely occurrences for which we must be vigilant.

'I don't like to use the word "cure" when it comes to treating any mental health problem because it assumes that there is some abnormality that must be eradicated, like a disease. Whereas to worry about our health is to be human. Again the problem is how much we do this and how much it interferes with living life. Also, given part of the problem for health anxious clients is the need to be guaranteed a clean bill of health, I think the term "cure" becomes even more problematic,' Saulsman writes.

'What I will say is that, with effective treatment, people can most definitely reduce how much they worry about their health, and people can stop living their life consumed with trying to prevent or detect physical illness and instead just start living life. It can be a lightbulb moment when clients realise that they are spending so much energy on trying to preserve their health but that these efforts are actually causing a poor quality of life. So they are trying so hard to stay alive, but the harder they try the more miserable their life becomes. A key message of therapy is that maybe they need to stop trying so hard.'

CBT-based therapies are the treatment of choice for health anxiety and teach those with it to address their thinking patterns (like focusing too much on internal sensations) and behaviour patterns (like reassurance seeking) that maintain their beliefs about the fragility of their health. For example, instead of being stuck in scary thoughts about your health, a therapist might teach you how to not push these thoughts or sensations closer, or push them further away, but instead postpone them to be revisited at a later time to reassess their true importance.

'One of the overarching themes across all anxiety disorders is difficulty tolerating uncertainty,' writes Dr Saulsman (and by now I am ready to ask her to adopt me). 'There are no guarantees with anything in life, and we have to live with that, tolerate that, and focus on living the best life we can. Therapy is about building that tolerance to uncertainty.'

And there are other techniques, ways to calm the raging fear that your bloody nose, diagnosed by a doctor as nothing more than the side effect of copping a cricket ball to the face, is actually a brain tumour.

Retraining attention is a solid way to start addressing health anxiety, especially if you hold any secret beliefs that focusing on your health is in some way protecting you – the old 'magical thinking' prevention.

One way to retrain attention is to practise focusing on mundane tasks. Often, when you are doing boring stuff like folding clothes or vacuuming, your mind wanders. But if you can practise focusing on what you are doing it is a great way to strengthen that ability: what does the vacuum sound like, how heavy is it, does it feel different on the carpet versus the wood floor, does it smell as it heats up, and so on. Strengthening this ability will help you to live in the present, rather than letting your mind sprint down the what-if rabbit hole of disease and misery.

Another practice is to work on reducing checking and reassurance seeking. We know that you might feel better for a bit if the doctor tells you that your fever is not malaria, but it is only a matter of time before you begin to fear it could be rabies and you are back at the doctor again, seeking something that will lift the weight of anxiety.

Health anxiety can be intense; more than intense – life ruining. The above is a sample of what an expert trained in helping those with health anxiety might do to help you feel better. And a professional, someone who has seen it before and knows how to guide you through the wasteland of terror, is the only way to get through an anxiety that feels like it could destroy you.

While I grew up misinterpreting, fixating upon and panicking about every real or imagined physical symptom I experienced, today it is the wellbeing of my children that can consume me. A lot of my health anxiety now is focused on my kids. Sometimes I don't know if I can get through another day as the worry is so intense, so real.

When I am having an episode, I will wake and, for just a moment, feel calm. But I am quickly overwhelmed by a feeling of dread. Could today be the day that something terrible happens to my babies? Will they start showing symptoms of something that can't be fixed?

When I drop my eldest at school and wave goodbye, on the outside I am smiling and happy to see him dash off to join the pack of kids torturing the assistant librarian, but on the inside every other child looks like a bag of germs, seething with viruses and bacteria and other nasties just waiting to jump on to my child to infect him with some vile, vomity disease.

The worst part of my health anxiety now – even though it has lessened greatly over the years, even though I can seek the evidence that shows that most of my ideas about illness are wrong – is that at times of intense stress, when the health anxiety finds the gaps to worm back through and curl its slimy tentacles around my heart, I feel so terrified that I wonder if my children would be far better off without me.

It passes, this feeling, it always passes, but when I am in it I always wonder if it will. If I should pack my bags and leave them with the sane parent who won't coddle them, annoy them, fill them with fear.

It is my deepest shame.

I can spend so much time worrying about my kids – if they are getting sick, if they are behaving normally, if they are happy – that it affects the way I treat them. And I fear I am making them afraid of living.

When I am anxious I will badger them to wash their hands before they eat; tell them off if they put their fingers in their mouths; if one of Sam's friends is away from school I will quiz him to find out why.

A few weeks ago his best friend was away on Monday but back on Tuesday. I asked Sam if he knew why and he said Max had 'bomited' in his bed. While he went off on a kid tangent about Max's mum having to clean it up and it being gross and funny, I was thinking about how long it would be before Sam started being sick, if I needed to ask his teacher if Max was still sick today and, after a few hours of this, whether I should just leave, for their sakes and for mine.

Sam didn't get sick.

Sometimes my health anxiety seems insurmountable. I don't know why everybody does not feel this way because it seems reasonable to me. The uncertainty is terrifying. I don't fear a friend not talking to me and I feel a normal amount of embarrassment if I say something dumb, because these things can't kill me. I am terrified of dying and, more than that, I am terrified of how destroyed I will be if my kids die or I have to watch them suffer. This has messed with my mind so badly that, at my worst, when the anxiety is so intense my body physically twists, I would rather not know them at all, would rather go far away and just let their dad and grandparents care for them and know, in my heart, that they are okay without having to be reminded constantly of the vacillations of human health and life. It is counterintuitive, it is completely stupid, but I love them so much and am so scared of losing them that sometimes I would rather they weren't in my life.

It is the most excruciating paradox.

This is the thing I am most disgusted of in myself. The stuff that makes me want to shrivel up. It is also what makes me question how much selfishness has to do with anxiety. I know I don't choose to feel this, to think this, but I am so worried about how the pain of my children would affect me that I imagine leaving them and being happier, carefree.

I had anxiety long before I had children. But thinking of leaving them, while I think it could be better for them, is not really about them at all. I wonder if it would be better for *me*.

I hate how unpredictable illness is, how messy. I hate that I can't plan anything as I am scared someone will get sick. The fear borders on superstition – that if I organise something I am inviting illness. That the universe is that much of an arsehole that it is waiting to surprise me and ruin all my plans.

You should have hung out with me when I was planning my wedding. I was a bloody joy.

12

Relationships

Emma, Rebecca and I stood around the rumpled bed, marvelling at the blob of semen on the sheets.

'It looks like Italy but bootier,' said Bec.

'Nope, I can see a face. See, that sticky-out bit is the nose,' said Emma.

'Is it meant to be that big?' I asked.

We considered it some more.

'It's gross though, right?'

We nodded emphatically.

The night before, as a mob of seventeen-year-olds staggered around the house somewhere on the scale between tipsy and vomiting, I had seen my first penis.

This was somewhat momentous as everyone else I knew had seen one (or seen loads) by then while I had spent my entire school career nodding sagely as friends described their latest sexual exploit with boys called Brett and Matt behind the bleachers at the Aquatic Centre.

To be fair, it's not like I was beating them off (with a stick!), but any boy who had shown the slightest interest up to this point had been swiftly fled from. There was the one at teen disco Pulse who had sent his mate over to ask me if I wanted to pash him. I had to ask the mate three times what he was saying because the music was very loud and the strobey lights were making me feel dizzy. Horrified, when I finally worked it out, I just went and stood behind the happy-pant-wearing teenagers throwing shapes in front of the bouncy castle. I saw his mate go and ask another girl straightaway.

There had been a boy on the bus who I was desperately in love with. Andrew Winters went to Pulteney Grammar and wore tight grey shorts and had a bit of black hair that hung over one eye. My best bus-friend, Lissy, thought he looked like a rat but I thought he was magnificent. So magnificent that, while he held court from the back of the bus, torturing younger kids and tagging the backs of seats with a magic marker, I sat up the front, heart thundering (this time with love), sneaking covert glances through the throngs of public school girls gathered around him, waiting for him to sweep them aside to ask me on a date to Fasta Pasta.

We got off at the same stop, as he lived just around the corner from our house – Mum said his dad would gallantly give her a lift up the hill when she was heavily pregnant – and I would follow twenty or so metres behind, watching his small bottom in his grey shorts, imagining all the lovely times we would have together when he eventually asked me to sit with him at the back of the bus.

Obviously never a word was spoken between us.

I did manage to eventually pash a boy at the very end of Year Twelve (with a closed mouth in a manner more like a pecking bird than an almost-grown human). He went to the local high school and had blond hair and a slow smile (that I eventually realised was because he was actually slow) and, of course, his name was Brett.

He kissed me outside a party, his face darting at mine before I knew what was happening, and then Mum drove up to get me and I pulled away, wide-eyed, and wiped my mouth. I was so thrilled by this I shook all night, waiting until 7 a.m. to ring all my friends to tell them. It's a safe bet that he wasn't as impressed, as next I heard he was going out with Headjob Holly and living in a caravan behind her folks' place.

Sean was my very first actual boyfriend. Emma and I met him and his friend at a pub we were too young to get into. Because he lived on one side of town and I on the other, he would only ever agree to pick me up from the city, so Mum, long-suffering Mum, would drive me in and drop me on the side of the road where he was slouching against a shop wall. Sauntering over, he would lean down and say something smooth to Mum through the open window, along the lines of 'don't you look lovely today and I promise to take good care of your daughter, *blah blah, suck*'. Mum would smile her small-teeth smile, give my arm a squeeze and tell me to give her a call when I needed to be picked up.

Being the self-involved teen I was, I had no compunction about calling her at midnight (or later) to say I was ready for my ride home. With buses to the hills stopping at 11 p.m. and having already failed the test for my learner's permit twice because I refused to read the training book (if it was meant to be, I would pass!), I had no other way home and I didn't consider actually catching that last bus home or reading the bloody training book. Mum would pick me up. And she always did.

Never drunk, because I was too scared alcohol would make me spew, I would nevertheless teeter moronically to Mum's car in my silly teen shoes, half an hour after I had told her I would come out to the car, and she would never say a word in complaint, and I would gaze moonily out the window while she drove us back up the winding roads home.

But on this particular night I had organised to stay at the place where Emma was house-sitting: a beautiful bluestone surrounded by roses and owned by an unsuspecting couple who believed her when she said she would just be writing uni assignments, and Sean was coming and I knew I would probably have to see him with his pants off, as he had been hinting at it for a while and I had run out of excuses. There is only so long you can say you have your period before even the most biologically illiterate boy starts to ask questions.

It was a hot night and I'd spent most of it avoiding Sean and hiding in corners, giggling, while my friends became increasingly irritated that I was stopping them from sloping off to the shadows with the greasy-haired boy of their choice.

Eventually, Sean cornered me with a shot of black Sambuca and I knew no other way to avoid what was coming. Following him to a bedroom, I shifted from foot to foot while his pants fell on the floor and he looked at me expectantly.

Thankfully, given he had been waiting for a long time and was only nineteen, it took only an experimental prod or two from my index finger before he defiled the sheets violently, accompanied by a dog-like grunt.

The relationship soon fizzled out. He moved to America on a scholarship and I cried myself to sleep, convinced he was the love of my life even though we had gone out for a mere two months and he was an only child whose mum refused to use my name and talked constantly about the nice Italian girl he would one day wed.

I am fickle when it comes to love. For many years, a man being interested in me was enough reason for me to dump them immediately. Even worse, if one showed vulnerability or, god forbid, nervousness, it was all over in a blink. If I felt that they depended on me in any way, needed me in any way,

I was repulsed. I always needed an escape plan, a clear path to a safe space, and if someone needed me I was trapped, suffocated.

I have only really been in love twice in my life, and I am married to the second. But I have been smitten countless times – heavily if the man in question was a big enough bastard. The more removed the man, the more I liked him. The less emotion he showed, the safer I felt.

Most of the men I dated were decent people – kind, sensitive, smart – and I found terrible reasons to break up with all of them. These include, in no particular order:

- Because he took too long to blink.
- Because he wore slip-on sandals and brought homemade artichoke dip to a party.
- Because he wrote poetry to my mum.
- Because he owned a black leather couch and called me his 'better half'.
- Because his leg hair was too dark.

Then I went out with one particularly mean man for far longer than I should have. I've since learned it is the charming ones you have to watch out for and, once clocked, avoid like the plague.

By the time I met him I had felt the sting of panic attacks, had known a truly broken heart, and had bounced back from the edge only to cling on to the first thing that walked past.

Marc was tall with a frighteningly hairy chest and he smelled like Lynx.

He was the one who would walk me to my car at the end of a night out, who made sure I had got home safely. Even though he had a girlfriend he hinted that it was all but over, she lived interstate and he was just waiting for the right time to break up with her.

Once I had decided that he was lovely, and as my heart started to dip, he became mean, nasty. Got angry if I spoke to any other men, bullied me until I stopped seeing any friends he didn't know; male friends I had known since childhood were out of the question.

He locked me out of his house one night because I danced with his friend at a club.

He yelled 'SLUT' in my face when I went to a male doctor and, when I fled his house, followed me in his car, screaming abuse.

I was only just emerging from the hollows, the fear of more panic attacks still swayed my head away from anything tough, and I thought being alone would be harder than staying with him.

One night he shook me hard when I argued back, and his flatmate saw – had walked out of his room at the wrong time – but he didn't say anything, just looked down and backed into his room.

I didn't dare tell Marc how anxious I was all the time back then. I don't think it is unfair to say he was too stupid to get it anyway. Too insecure to think of the pain others might be going through, so intensely interested was he in not being bettered by another man.

Thankfully he finally broke up with me when he found someone else to go out with. When I didn't seem as upset as he would have liked he started ringing again, asking me to go to movies or to dinner, but I knew, finally knew, that I was better off alone.

Instead of being ignored by him in his lounge at night, I would sit at home with my flatmate Amy and we would drink wine as I told her all the horrible things he had done and we laughed at how stupid I had been but, even more, at what an arsehole he was, and it all seemed fine when couched in the haze of our comfy lounge room.

I met Amy behind the counter of our local Bakers Delight; she was the one who found it as hard to rouse an encouraging smile when describing the merits of Apricot Delight over Pullapart (we were firm pullapart devotees, would accidentally--on-purpose drop a spinach and feta one so we could eat it slyly behind the racks) as I did.

Amy was also prone to bouts of paranoid obsession, and we bonded over Oasis and boys with shaggy hair and *Who* magazine. Over the years – we have known each other for almost two decades – we have travelled together and lived together; she is the godmother of my first child. She was also the friend I could most depend upon to not look at me like I was a complete mental when I confessed my latest paranoia. No stranger to odd phobias – I wasn't allowed to make toast in our house as it made her feel like she was having a stroke – Amy and I revolved around each other like unstable planets.

Until my husband, the people I found who could best handle my dark side, my ugly anxiety, were other women. Some sucked, sure; some looked at me like I was completely mad and offered stupid advice like 'drink more green tea' or 'just stop worrying'. But, mostly, my female friends didn't mind if I sobbed into the arm of their couch or if I went dangerously quiet on a night out, and would share their own worries, fears, darkness, ugliness. It was a comfort to be able to look into the eyes of another, to share your fear that he shook you because you were disgusting and stupid, and to have her hug you and then laugh and show you that your fear was not real, your anxiety not manifest. To have a soft place to rest when it all gets more than you can keep holding in your head.

A problem shared, when that problem is anxiety, really is a problem halved. To hear the fears of others, especially when they mirror your own, is to step out of the shadows. You are not alone. You are not a freak. You are human, that is all.

Just don't spend too much time with the arseholes.

Other Stories

She always seems serene to me. Tall and graceful, O speaks quietly so you have to lean close to hear her.

Anxiety feels like a crushing weight on my chest that invades my entire being. It feels like a million angry insects flying through my veins. It feels like my heart is going to burst out of my chest, and the arteries in my neck are going to explode. It feels like my heart doesn't know how to pump any more, and is probably sending me into arrest right now. It feels like I can never get enough air. It feels like a feeling of dread consuming me, this knowledge that somehow everything is going to go horribly wrong and there's nothing I can do to stop it. It feels hot and burning. It feels cold and heavy. It feels like I'm trapped and there's no escape and there's no option but for me to check out and hope for the best. Anxiety puts me in the freeze response.

So many things can cause anxiety for me. The report of a war in a foreign country tells me that planes will soon be flying overhead, dropping bombs on my children. A 'look' from someone tells me that I'm messing up again. Sometimes I don't even know. It just floods me and I'm there, again.

Breathing helps me stay alive. Deep, slow breaths. Meditating helps a lot, but I have to keep reminding myself that any thought (ANY THOUGHT) is okay, it doesn't mean anything, let it go. I keep focusing on the space and let the thoughts pass by. Talking to someone who won't try and 'fix' me or judge me is helpful. Sometimes I just need to get it out of my head and speak it out. Sometimes I have to move – walk, dance, shake – just to get it out. Laughing helps. Even a maniacal forced laugh. Eventually I'll start laughing properly and that helps. Screaming helps too. Burying my face into my husband's shoulder and screaming it all out.

I've had anxiety since I was a child. I just didn't know it until I was twenty-six because mental health disorders were unacceptable in my family, and therefore didn't exist.

Acknowledgement, and acceptance, are key to facing and lessening anxiety. Don't wait for the people around you to give you permission to have anxiety. If you know that something is up, talk to a doctor or psychologist.

I started to truly believe there was something inherently wrong with me — something disgusting, that the words anxiety had whispered in my ear all those years were really true.

13

Performance anxiety

Very early on I realised that the key to happiness and popularity would be to become famous.

From my earliest moments, I lived as if a greater audience was watching. The diary I kept as a scrawny and boobless nine-year-old was written as though it would be dug up by future civilisations who would use it as evidence of how sophisticated 1980s Australian girls were.

At ten, after years of badgering, I was finally allowed to visit an acting agent because I knew they would meet me and immediately stick me on the telly. I wore my very best floor-length denim skirt with the red-and-white rugby jumper I saved for special occasions. Patent leather slip-ons with lace-edged ankle socks and a long lace ribbon tied to a shank of my boy-short hair, feathered in the fashion of the day, rounded out my outfit. There is a photo, which I have taken pains to hide, of me doing a Marilyn Monroe pose, hand on alluringly jutted hip; Mum snapped it with her Polaroid just before we left to catch the bus to town. You can see the youthful hope shining in my eyes – the hope that was dimmed, but not destroyed, when the agent said she would love to sign me up if only we paid 200 dollars for a portfolio first.

Even if we had been able to afford the portfolio, I doubt the results would have been terribly useful. While I could bust a saucy Marilyn at home, there was no way I could have done anything more than stare gormlessly at the camera if a stranger was asking me to pose.

With acting megastardom out of the question – at least until I could find a way to raise portfolio coin – I instead focused my attention on getting a famous boyfriend.

Many happy hours were spent imagining the limo coming up the long drive at school. The door would swing open and I would step out to gasps of appreciation – no, idolisation. Then, in glorious slow motion, Christian Slater would rise from the car, hair draped over one eye while the other was trained only on me, his adoration clear for all to see. By this stage the entire school would be gathered around the car, cool kids in front where I could study them for signs of jealousy up close, and they would turn as one as we walked up the steps, bound for the principal's office so I could tell him about how rich and successful I was and he would put me on the cover of the newsletter. Sometimes the local TV stations would land on the oval in their helicopters too.

In his book *The Meaning of Anxiety*, Rollo May remarks that he observed a group of young women with neurotic anxiety who were all from the middle class. Essentially, he blames the disparity between the expectations of the middle class and their reality, and that the subsequent competitive ambition is linked with modern anxiety.[1]

My family could not be more firmly middle class if we tried, much to the disappointment of my more romantic self, who imagines that writing a book would be much easier if I was struck down with consumption in some back alley walk-up or lying about in my harem being handfed oysters by frustrated castratos. Us poor middle class lack the true struggle faced by the proletariat, the grit borne of lining up in picket lines down at the wharf or being forced to watch our mums wrestle others for formula at the rundown Coles at the end of the road, yet we are also hamstrung by the lack of cash available to the upper class, who can make even more money and enjoy epic success despite the lack of any discernible talent. (I'm looking at you, Kardashians.)

After some careful thought, I realised I probably wouldn't be able to orchestrate a meeting with Christian Slater while I was still at school (because obviously a meeting is all it would have taken – one look and he would have been smitten), so I was forced back to more traditional options.

At thirteen I signed up to take acting lessons (god only knows how many baskets of ironing Mum had to do to afford them) with a local talent agency despite not having any actual obvious talent and suffering from extreme shyness and performance anxiety.

I auditioned to be Paul Robinson's long-lost daughter on *Neighbours* and was devastated when I didn't get a call-back as I had already decided what I would wear when I won the Gold Logie and Bruce Samazan (of *E Street* fame) asked me to marry him.

When one of the actors from the show came to talk to our class I was so desperate to make a good impression that I put on way too much tinted pimple cream, got hives all over my cheek and spent the session hiding behind my jumpered-hand. He did not propose.

I had always sung, spent many interminable car rides to pointless childhood destinations like the Maritime Museum warbling Whitney Houston songs while I viciously pinched whichever brother was unfortunate enough to get stuck in the middle seat.

When I finished school I knew that I didn't want to go to uni – fame did not lie that way – so I enrolled at the local TAFE in a music course, because music is a sure-fire way to vast riches.

Having to sing in front of people, though – kind of an important part of being an actual singer – was something I wasn't at all prepared for. I spent a large portion of the year I studied singing actually avoiding singing. Despite this, despite not practising and often being physically unable to hit a note, any note, during performances because I was engulfed in terror, I ended up in a band.

Called Molecule and desperate to be some kind of renegade funk-acid-jazz outfit, the band was made up of me, usually unable to face forwards during a performance and often drowned out by the drums and ludicrously loud bass anyway; a hairy Russian called Vlad whose face I never fully saw, I just caught glimpses of doughy cheeks and stubble-pimples through his thick thatch of face-covering curls; a balding drummer on whom I had a crush because he was the one I thought was least likely to corner me in a dark alleyway after a gig; Richard, who was the band leader and mostly complained about Vlad; and one other whose name escapes me but he had glasses and receding hair and a voice that I couldn't hear even when the others had stopped playing. I can only assume he played the keys.

Somehow, thanks to the one or two gigs I shouted my way through while hiding behind Vlad, I got a job with another band who were leaving to play in mainland China for a year.

I was twenty, grossly naive, way too gullible, and desperate to go even though I was scared to death. Mum and Dad asked the manager, who was also the bass player of the band (what is it with bass players?), to come to the house so they could check him out.

I think they believed that if they met him face to face, they would be able to tell if he was a serial killer or planned to sell me into a prostitution ring, like that kind of depravity is something people wear on their outsides.

Tall and hook nosed, Mario was as smooth as they come. He sat on the low couch, drank Mum's tea and explained that he would look out for me, make sure I was okay. Mum rang the music union to make sure he was above board, spent an hour asking them questions and seeking assurances.

So off I went, just me and five Australian men who turned out to be some of the most misogynistic, racist dickheads to ever don a pair of leather pants.

Six days a week we performed at Hard Rock Cafes across China, singing classic hits like 'Macarena' and 'YMCA' while drunk Chinese businessman tried to distract me with large wads of yuan equivalent to around $2.40 as they grabbed at my bottom.

I entered into a very ill-advised relationship with the male singer of the band, a sly pervert who had hair like Cher, wore cowboy boots, and harboured a desperate need to be urinated upon (before you ask, the answer is no).

The pervert and I shared a room in Guangzhou, our tiny beds covered in Garfield sheets, the mattresses actually filled with straw. The band that had been there before us left a welcoming note on the table just inside the door of the apartment, only reached after climbing twenty-two floors as the lift sometimes worked but usually did not.

The note, scrawled on a damp bit of paper torn from an exercise book, read 'Welcome to Shitsville, ha ha ha ha'.

Looking back it seems like a mostly unfunny teen movie – the sex-obsessed men, the bad music, the burgers and beer. It is also the point at which I started to come unstuck.

For the twenty years leading up to this, if I was unsure or anxious or scared or confused, I had someone to turn to, someone to lean on. Too trusting, too naive and too gullible, I turned to the men in the band to provide me with stability, with reassurance, and this was a very bad idea.

It was easy, really, for them to make me feel awful. I was isolated, scared, and didn't have any idea how to relate to men a lot older than me. Things started to go bad very quickly. Mario decided I wasn't performing well enough and would berate me at the end of every night, pointing out, with derision, all the ways I had stuffed up, not been good enough. Part of the contract was that the venue would feed us every day but he decided that, at fifty-five kilograms, I was getting too fat, and he ordered the other band members to watch what I ate, ordered the waitstaff not to bring me anything other than salads.

The ill-advised relationship failed when Cher's girlfriend turned up – although he had said something along the lines of there being no girlfriend – and he stopped talking to me. My bed was moved into the lounge, so I couldn't sleep until the others had stopped drinking and decided to finally crash. Then my pay was cut because apparently I still wasn't performing well enough and didn't deserve even the shitty amount I was being paid.

If any of this happened now I would give them a vicious two-fingers and bugger off, but I was so young and too embarrassed to go home a failure.

We moved to Beijing and lived in a hotel where I had to share a room with the fat guitarist and his weird Canadian girlfriend, had to listen to them doing all sorts of revolting things while I shoved my head under the pillow and hummed to drown them out.

As well as playing, we had to socialise with the punters in between sets and afterwards. Usually this was fine, as most people were polite, but there was one man who hung around more and more often.

Sanjeet owned cruise ships or hotels or something. I didn't know or care what he did and just tagged along when he took the band out for drinks after the show. When it was hot and the sleeve of his shirt slipped up I could see an R seared on to his bicep with cigarette burns. He was way older than me, fifty at least, and I sat at the other end of the table, quietly, as the others drank and laughed loudly and said revolting things in English about the Chinese girls serving us food.

One night Mario, who was really just an inordinately sleazy guy with crooked teeth who liked to sleep spread-eagled on his bed with the door open and no pants on, pulled me aside to tell me that Sanjeet had a proposition.

'He wants you to be his concubine. He will buy you an apartment, set you up on the Gold Coast or somewhere, and all you have to do is be around when he is in Australia,' Mario said.

'It's a really good opportunity for a woman.'

I honestly didn't think he was serious. Thought it was some kind of stupid man-joke that I just didn't get. But a couple of nights later, after another interminable evening spent sitting around a table watching everyone get drunk, Mario asked me to help walk Sanjeet home.

We got him to his hotel door, watched him unlock it, and Mario gave me a swift shove from behind, propelling me forwards on to the bed.

Sanjeet sat down beside me as I shrank against the headboard.

'So, have you thought about it,' he said, 'thought about what I can give you?'

I'm not an idiot – I knew it would be better not to offend him in a country where keeping face is so important, especially as I didn't know where in the city I was or if anyone could hear me.

I sat very still, small as a mouse.

'Thank you very much for the offer,' I whispered. 'It is very kind, but I am the kind of person who would like to make it on her own.'

He nodded, seemed to accept my answer, let me walk out to the hallway where Mario was leaning against the wall. When I told Mario I had said no he sneered and said I was stupid.

I thought it was all over but a couple of nights later Sanjeet was back, watching us play, drinking, buying drinks. Somebody invited him back to our hotel and he followed the fat guitarist into our room, to talk or do whatever it is drunk men do. But instead he sat beside me on my bed, started pulling at my clothes while the others laughed.

One band member – I can only assume it was the keyboardist as he had a shred of the decency the others so badly lacked – distracted him as I fled to the room next door, where the drummer's girlfriend was about to go to sleep. I cried on her shoulder as she shooshed and hugged me. I listened as her boyfriend came into the room and she yelled at him for being an arsehole while he complained about my tears.

Not long afterwards, maybe a week or two, we were at dinner when Mario told me I would be leaving the next day. He already had another singer lined up, a teen from the Philippines (poor thing), and my flight was booked for first thing the following morning. I am ashamed that I cried again, asked what I had done wrong and if I could come back on another tour.

How I have imagined, countless times since, standing up and calling them all arseholes, telling them all exactly what I thought of them and what cowardly men they were. I have imagined leaving months before it even got this far, storming out the first time I was told I was shit, head and two fingers held high.

I want to go back in time and kick that girl in her soft gut and yell, 'STAND UP FOR YOURSELF! FIGHT BACK! WHAT ARE YOU DOING?'

But instead I slunk out of China in the grey dawn, caught a taxi while the others slept, not even one of those bastards getting up to say goodbye.

Mum says that when she saw me get off the plane I was smaller, my shoulders tipped in to meet each other, slumped. Back at home after nine months away, my room felt small and I tortured myself with all the things I could have done differently, berated myself for not being a different person, the kind of person Mario and the others would have liked, respected.

I started to truly believe there was something inherently wrong with me – something disgusting, that the words anxiety had whispered in my ear all those years were really true.

That it was something I could avoid, stop, if I just listened more closely to the skipping-beat of my heart, the warning fired deep in my belly.

I always felt like I was missing out on something, that I was wasting time, totally incapable of committing myself to the moment, always thinking of the future and fearing a bad one.

14

Travel

It is a particularly annoying and painful truism of my life that I despise travel but keep making myself go places.

I love imagining the places I can go, thinking about the kind of person I will be when I get there. I imagine lying, carefree and bronzed, under palm trees, hiking unsweatily through a rainforest while marvelling at its beauty and, perhaps, prettily shedding a tear when a baby monkey jumps onto my shoulder, to the great surprise and delight of the guide who assures me (in his native tongue as I have picked it up in a week) that he has never before seen a *gringa* with such a natural affinity for the land.

I dream about wandering the streets of New York, haggling for local jewellery at street markets in Africa, tending wounded wildlife in Borneo where I will doze off, at the end of a long day, in a hammock that looks over a misted valley, a baby orangutan tucked under each arm, a frosted G&T in my hand and a platter of local delicacies at my side as I have been blessed with a gut that can handle even the rarest of delicacies without explosive protest.

But, without fail, I am the one who will spend the night before a departure gripped with panic that the plane will crash, Googling local diseases, sitting on hold to the airlines trying to work out how much money it will cost me to cancel three hours before take-off.

I am the one who will get the crook guts despite drinking only bottled water and eating well-cooked food. I am the one who worries about local crime, ferry capsizes, tsunamis, Ebola, and will stay up late at night reading horrific *Daily Mail* stories about Westerners who have died terrible deaths while on their dream holidays.

And yet I persist.

The idea of travelling and being able to look back rose-coloured-glassily – once the discomfort and stress and catastrophising have ebbed – almost makes the pain of actually going somewhere worth it.

I have an unerring ability to remember things without the horrible parts. Perhaps this talent for suppression is partly why my anxiety is so tenacious. Every time it rears its head it feels like the first time. The terror and clenching and fixating feel fresh and if they are new then they must mean something bad is about to happen.

Then the anxiety passes and I gladly push it aside and only think about what a nice time I have had.

I remember idyllic trips to tiny Australian towns with my family, traipsing through main streets, clambering through scrub looking for lakes, gorging on fish and chips and sausage rolls full of tomato sauce, before dropping quickly into sleep every night. But if I think about it just a little harder I will get a knife in the gut as I vividly picture myself edging down the narrow path on Mt Schank at Mt Gambier, having ventured into the base of the extinct volcano with my dad and brother because I was desperate to be part of the fun while ignoring the plaintive wail of my already dangerously full bladder, which finally decided to relieve itself halfway down the hill. Now I see myself pushing my back to the rock wall as wave after wave of tourists passes us as I try to hide my hot pink–trousered bottom, now dark pink with urine. I remember slipping into the back seat of the car, shame-faced and quiet, not wanting Mum or Dad to know that their disgusting eight-year-old daughter had pissed her pants.

The first time I ever flew – a trip to Brisbane to visit a badly thought-out boyfriend who had decided to chuck in his job as a chef to become a dancer – is remembered as a month-long road trip of delight, all steamy sunsets, beach barbecues and rainforest exploring. But then I think a bit harder and behind the bullshit was the first night we spent on Fraser Island when, miles from any way of getting off said island and away from said boyfriend, he decided to tell me that he had cheated with some girl he met at a Pantera concert. And the next morning when I woke up covered in a rash – a combination of stress and midge bites – that he had absolutely no sympathy for and which sent me scurrying for a public phone, where I rang Mum, crying, so she could ring the doctor to find out what might be going on and to assure me that I wasn't about to die.

There is a biological reason why it is harder to remember the particulars of stressful times. Cortisol, the hormone your body releases during stress, prevents the formation of memories. You also tend to be a little distracted during an anxiety attack so the details of what is happening are difficult to retain – you might not even notice them.

And yet I persist.

Like all twenty-something Australians convinced they are destined for something greater – or who just like drinking with wild abandon far away from anyone who will tell them to stop – I eventually headed for London with the boyfriend I thought I would spend my forever with.

I had met Andy the year before, first saw him at a party, his blond head shining poetically in the fly-fogged lights. I thought I saw him staring at me but, just home from China and still epically messed up, I figured there was no way that was actually the case. It was.

When we finally spoke, weeks later, when I saw him at a bar and told him he had chewing gum stuck to his pants (smooth), he told me he had been thinking about me since that first night. We swapped numbers, he promised to ring. I woke the next morning not believing he actually would – still believing what Mario and his cronies had thought of me – but he did, just that morning, and we went to a football game and ate chips and yelled laughing abuse at the players.

I thought he was the most beautiful thing I had ever seen. He was gentle and thoughtful, ran me a bath one night when I was late home from uni, covered the surface with rose petals like we were in a bad teen movie, and then cooked me dinner while I lowered myself in. We were twenty-one.

At the end of that year, happy again and confident and filled with purpose and the feeling that it was him and me against the world, like something I had read in all those books was finally happening to me, we set off overseas, waving our parents goodbye at the airport with flippant promises that we wouldn't see them for *years* and I remember Mum's face being sad but smiling so I wouldn't worry.

We started in Malaysia, where we swam and explored, and I worried a little about eating the local food. Once in London we decided to buck convention and find jobs in pubs, and I auditioned for a German girl band – my very first audition in

Europe – and I was offered the gig. *I'm not shit!* I thought. It felt like redemption, a chance to prove to myself, but mostly to those men left behind in China, that I was better, better than them.

Andy came with me for the first week in the tiny German town where the band was based. The producer – who was not at all sleazy and kindly put us up in his beautiful home – had me run through some of the songs while we waited for the two other girls in the band to arrive. That week, besides the few times I had to sing a song for a record exec or two, was spent exploring the town, eating chips doused in mayonnaise and tomato sauce with tiny plastic forks, going to taverns for giant schnitzels, and waking up to breakfasts of orange juice and salami.

But after a week Andy went back to London to work and things started to fall apart. The other girls arrived and they were tiny identical twins who danced like infernos and didn't say a whole lot. We started to practise dance routines that they would make up on the spot and I would feel completely ridiculous while trying to keep up. I was so much taller than them and looked like a giant marionette being operated by someone with a head injury.

I worried that Andy was meeting other girls and deciding they were much nicer than me, and called him a lot to see if I could pick any change in his voice over the phone. I whined to the producer about whether the project was really right for me, as though I had so many others waiting in the wings, but when he finally said he didn't think it was working out, I freaked and tried to bribe my way back in. But I was also relieved that I didn't have to stay in this place where I knew no one and had to put on a happy face (which I was obviously doing a very crap job of) when inside I was an insecure mess.

Back in London I got a job in a bar, although I was disconcerted by how quickly Andy had made a whole swag of new friends. At his bar after work he was surrounded by admirers who talked about the parties he had thrown while I was away (it was a week, who is that determined?) and I glared at them sullenly.

As much as other people seemed to relish the chance to just 'be' while in London, to drink and laugh and hang out and travel, I always felt like I was missing out on something, that I was wasting time, totally incapable of committing myself to the moment, always thinking of the future and fearing a bad one.

For reasons that remain unknown (pity?) the German producer recommended me for another project, this time in Spain. And the same thing happened. I was desperately lonely, didn't understand what anyone was saying and forgot to take any books with me, so I spent hours every day walking around the compound where I was staying. The band was being put together by a man who had made an unseemly amount of money selling fake watches and had decided he wanted to crack the Western music market even though he didn't play an instrument or speak English.

The two other girls in the band were Spanish and didn't speak a word of English either. I felt ridiculously white and boring; when they whipped off their bikini tops on the beach I sat there like a lump of tapioca in my singlet, watching their worldliness with envy.

And again I changed my mind and begged to be sent home, until they sent me home and I changed my mind, again.

Andy and I were in London for about two years before things started to go seriously south. I had my first panic attack, out of the blue, and it scared me more than anything before it ever had. One panic attack became two became countless. Because I didn't know what they were, had no idea what was going wrong with me or even how to properly describe it, I got quieter and quieter, my mind busily thinking of all the things I needed to avoid in order to stay safe.

There are entire trips – to Athens, Barcelona, Scotland – that I barely remember, so intent was I on trying to keep my shit together.

Andy and I began to fight over stupid things, the ultimate clichés: he would yell at me for trying to control him and I would yell at him for being a selfish prick.

He went on a 'boys trip' (ick) to Greece and, to spite him, I organised my own trip and left before he got back. For one week I panicked about dying on a random Greek island, spent most of the sunny days in our hotel room while my friends went to the beach, imagined sudden allergies to foods I had always eaten and became too scared to try much more than yoghurt dip and chips.

When I arrived home Andy was shame-faced (I didn't want to know why) and had made a photo album of all of our 'happiest' moments away. It just felt so stilted and forced and wrong, and I was so unhappy but desperate for him to stay. His best friend had proposed to his girlfriend while we were away and I felt sick that Andy might get a funny idea and ask me the same, because in no way did I want to marry him, but I knew that I would collapse, sink into myself, if he left.

He did not ask.

I knew Andy didn't want to be with me any more but he seemed to be sticking around through the last shreds of a sense of duty to not dump a girl who was losing her shit. It felt like the beauty of us had disappeared, leaving a murky stain, a cheap knock-off of what we had once been and I hated myself, blamed myself for everything. Even in my messed-up state I could tell he wanted out – he wasn't trying terribly hard to hide it. I was a burden, a trial, a pain in his overseas sojourn, annoying and embarrassing in my need, too needy for a 24-year-old man.

I organised a final trip away from London, before my visa expired and I thought we would both be heading home, to try to fix what was so very broken.

He was there but not for most of the trip. He forgot to renew his driver's licence before we left for a road trip across the United States, sleeping next to me from Seattle to Atlanta as I white-knuckled it and swallowed the panic, feeling sorry for myself and furiously frightened at him.

The anxiety during this trip was so intense that it is almost too much to remember, no matter how hard I try. I know I thought I was going crazy. I know I was exhausted. I know I was desperate to make him love me again.

Make him love me again, as if this is ever possible.

Hardly able to walk to the car in the morning and at risk of going to sleep as I drove the long stretches of tedious grassland in the American Midwest, the trip was a grotesque adventure in self-hatred come to life.

I drove through small town after small town, past mouldering trailer parks thick with overweight people and crying children. Flashes of staying night after night in small roadhouses and crappy motels where the manager was inevitably white and suspicious.

Giving a lift to a black couple in Kansas City who warned us, straightaway, to never give anybody a lift ever again.

Dragging myself through Graceland, exhausted and annoyed by the sobbing Americans around Elvis's grave.

The further we drove, the thinner I got, unable to eat and engulfed by panic attacks and dread and desperation. I could see myself doing the same trip if I was a different kind of person, laughing and drinking and making friends, instead of sleeping in the car while Andy talked to the cowboys at the bar in South Dakota, hiding in the motel room when he eventually woke up and went in search of greasy food.

In Florida we stayed with a friend of his aunt's – a man who was more beard than flesh – who kept an automatic gun under his bed and liked to point out all the ways we were stupid. But he let us stay in his house by the canal where, finally able to stop driving, I got sick and lay in bed for four days with some horrid stomach virus and strep throat, which was diagnosed by a dishearteningly good-looking blond doctor who flirted with Andy while scraping my throat with a swab. I gagged and tried not to look pathetic.

I remember wanting to make him happy. Wanting him to want to be with me. Once the meds kicked in and I stopped throwing up, he talked me into going for a ride to the beach to watch the sunset. I was so tired that I was having trouble walking but I hoped he wouldn't notice as I wanted to be vital and carefree, like young travellers in love are supposed to be. I remember leaning back against him, while surfers surfed and golden girls laughed, and I tried to slow my breathing and quell the shakes.

Constant dread, that is what I felt. That death was imminent, I just didn't know from where. What I wanted was to not feel this way, to be normal, but if that wasn't possible then I wanted to crawl into a hole where I could be safe, where everything could be controlled, where he wouldn't leave me and I couldn't catch a terrible illness or be hit by a car or kidnapped or stabbed.

The further south we got, the more I lost my grip on reality.

Driving west across Texas, my body tensed when Andy suggested we explore the desert on foot. We found an abandoned town and I was too scared to get out of the car because it felt so bad that I honestly began to believe in the supernatural, that a mob of blackened and oozing vampires would swarm from the buildings, dragging us away.

Night after night, in town after shitty town, all with different names but all depressingly and disorientatingly the same, I would struggle to explore these new places. And it was all so unfair. Why couldn't I be like all the others? I wanted to shake this young woman and scream in her wilted face, 'JUST BE NORMAL! JUST BE SOMEONE ELSE! HE IS LEAVING YOU! WHY WOULD HE STAY?'

In San Diego I watched people compete in an ultramarathon on the television and they were sweating and somewhere hot and, for the first time, it occurred to me that if I watched them get too hot I might die too. There was no reason that I would make this association, yet the dread dripped through my bones.

As Andy changed to go back outside for dinner I cowered on the floor, pretending to play a game but really too terrified to move and entirely aware that the fear I was feeling watching people get sweaty on TV was irrational – but what if it wasn't? What if it were proof that I was losing my mind, but what if it wasn't? And I couldn't stop it and I couldn't tell anyone what my brain was doing and I had no choice but to grin and put my new shoes on and try to marvel at the new city and food and try not to fade away.

We crossed the border into Mexico and my heat phobia began to paralyse me. There is a photo of me in Sayulita, a seaside town and firm favourite of surfers. I am smiling and as brown-as-I-can-get, one hand dangling over a plate of guacamole, the ubiquitous Corona in the other, under some kind of tropical tree, and all I can see is someone desperately trying to hold it together.

It was in Sayulita that I got sick again, properly sick. I had a fever and I was hallucinating. I lay on the beach covered in the striped blanket I bought that day and I saw a pirate galleon sailing overhead, canons cocked, sails fluttering, set darkly against the stars.

Staggering back to our tent I was wracked with cramps and I was sick in every way a person can be while Andy slept. I asked for help but I had asked for help too many times to count and he was tired and sick of me.

The next day, having found a local to drive us to the nearest town, I rang Mum once again. Small-voiced down the phone, I asked her to ring the doctor once again, to find out what could be done for me. She called back with advice to buy a big bottle of Coke and to add salt to it to stave off dehydration, as I didn't have any hydrolite and couldn't imagine trying to find a chemist.

Now used to my excuses, Andy went out alone. He didn't even say where he was going any more, just jammed his pack with a bottle of water and his wallet and headed out the door. I saw him again when the sun went down. Sometimes not even then. He was making friends with other travellers. With other girls.

By the time we made it to Acapulco I was agoraphobic. This might seem an exaggeration, as I hadn't locked myself away in my house for months or years at a time the way agoraphobics do in movies or late-night crazy-person porn. But I had become so panic stricken that I could not leave the hotel room. As he went on adventures or lay by the pool, I lay on the bed with the fan on full, wiping my face with wet towels, trying to slow my heart while my brain chanted *deathdeathdeath*.

If only my heart would slow, I thought, I might be able to get outside, to do something, anything. But it was beating so furiously that this must have been proof that it was weak and couldn't handle this heat. Andy managed to coax me out once or twice, only to glare at me and bark, 'Hurry up', as I walked very slowly down the road, bent like an old woman, trying desperately to slow my heart.

Back in London, all I did was cry and sleep and all he did was yell.

My visa expired and I had to leave, and wanted to more than anything, but I despised the thought of going home. And he wouldn't come with me, said he needed just a couple more months in the city, a couple more working and making money and then he would come home and we would be together, move on together.

I flew home, tucked tightly into myself, not speaking a word, trying not to remember how Andy pulled his shoulders back in relief as he walked away from me at Heathrow.

Mum and Dad met me at the airport and they grabbed me in enormous hugs, and with plastered-grins asked me how the trip was even though they could see I was small and shrunken.

Walking into my room, it was the same room I had left three years before but everything had changed in me and nothing had changed there. The same posters were on the wall, the same blue quilt, the same clutter. I sat in the middle of the bed, feet on the same blue carpet squares that had been there since I was a baby, and the heaviness in my chest felt like it would drag me under the floor – and I wanted it to. I didn't want to take another breath. I wanted to sleep until I felt better but I didn't know how that would ever be, how I could live a normal day knowing what could happen, that a panic attack could come from nowhere and tear me apart while people watched and did nothing.

And, more than anything, I longed for Andy. I crossed off the days on a calendar, marking the moments until he would come home. I wanted to shut my eyes and not open them until he was with me.

Andy called every few days and I tried to make my voice light and tell him all the things I was doing, all the things I was capable of doing, none of which were true. I spoke of friends and adventures and study, and he listened and then he became distracted and the calls become fewer and then it was only me calling.

A week before he was due to come home he rang and I could hear laughter in the background and he was laughing too, and he told me he was not coming back.

And I wondered how I would survive.

•

Because panic attacks can mimic real heat stress, having a panic response or phobia to heat is not uncommon. Like panic attacks, heat stress can make your heart beat rapidly, make you nauseous, dizzy and sweaty.

My panic attacks were happening multiple times every day when Andy and I visited the US and because I didn't have a name for them at that stage and I was too scared to see a doctor, I interpreted my feelings of panic as symptoms of heat stroke. So to my poor addled brain, feeling those symptoms when watching someone sweating on TV was evidence enough that my body's inability to tolerate heat was so extreme that even seeing someone feeling hot could be enough to kill me.

Of course, my rational brain knew this was silly, that there was no chance that this could be true. *But what if,* that little voice whispered – *what if?* Surely it was better to be safe than sorry, to stay inside, near showers and water and air-conditioning and a phone, just in case.

Classic avoidance, again – anxiety's sordid partner in crime.

Medication, for me, was key in getting rid of my heat phobia. By the time I sought help the panic attacks were so frequent and so severe, the physical symptoms so overwhelming, that I couldn't even discuss trying CBT and its attendant exposure therapy, although it was one of the first things the psychologist I saw tried.

However, medication, when we eventually hit upon the right one for me, dulled my physical response to panic enough that I could start to test myself in scary situations and begin to recognise that the symptoms I had felt (but didn't feel on the medication) in hot situations must have been due to anxiety and not because my body fundamentally couldn't handle being hot.

Cognitive therapies can work very well but until the adrenaline stopped banging through my body, rattling my bones, threatening to blow off the top of my head at a time when I would have welcomed it, there was no way for me to even begin.

Many people with anxiety are afraid to take drugs. They think the drugs will change their personality, that what they feel won't be authentic, that the side effects will make the benefits pale. I thought all of those things and more; I still wanted to believe I could control myself with my mind if only I tried harder, if I stopped being so useless.

Other Stories

There is an ex-girlfriend of a dear friend. She has a big grin and talks a mile a minute, asks lots of questions and actually listens when you answer.

Depression seems to run in my family; however, I seem to run a slippery slope that starts with anxiety and leads to depression and I have even had the triumvirate of anxiety, agoraphobia and depression together – glad to have crawled out of that hole!

These days I don't have anxiety 'attacks' in the way that people would normally think of them, like the instant hit of freaking out and hyperventilating, which is why I thought I would write you as I'm sure there are others with very different 'anxiety attacks' and we should get it all out there because it does prevent me from behaving kinda normal!

My anxiety attacks can be triggered by something as simple as knowing I have to have an uncomfortable conversation with an employee. But that is just the trigger because then I get into what I think of as The Spiral. I am anxious about the uncomfortable conversation but it is trickling into lots of other thoughts.

In the daytime I become quite paranoid, irrationally freaking out about my children's safety. I can't sleep because I am hashing and rehashing past friends and relationships, thinking that I handled them badly, I have wronged people, I am basically not a very nice person.

My husband knows I am spiralling because I start to bite my lip until it is basically destroyed. Let's call a spade a spade here, that pain is some kind of distraction for me from the spiralling anxiety and so it is some kind of coping mechanism, though not a good one. So, anyway, an 'anxiety attack' can last for a week or two weeks. If the trigger can be resolved quickly, that is good, but it still might take time to spiral out of the anxiety.

Coping strategies, did I hear you ask? Trying to rise above it early. If I treat the lip-biting as the canary in the coal mine, then I try to think of things I could do to help friends and family to get out of my own head. I'm learning to play the ukulele, which can sometimes help as a distraction. I don't think I have that many strategies, I just keep telling myself that it will pass.

I read this thing lately that said that people who suffer from anxiety and depression are not weak, it is actually that they have been tough for too long! I think that is true, and it is also why we are so good at putting on a brave face a lot of the time. I'm always freaking out that my children are going to be stolen. And when I am anxious about anything, it makes me act like a loon about keeping them near – as if no one can keep an eye on them like I can. But honestly, if someone took my son, they would have a couple of nights of no sleep thanks to his nocturnal habits and perhaps they would return him.

I don't think my children are going to be stolen but I, too, have acted like a loon around them. Maybe all parents do it and those of us with anxiety just let our imaginations go too far sometimes.

15

Superstition and magical thinking

I know there are those out there who relish chaos, who like to fly by the seat of their pants, not knowing what each day will bring.

I am not that person.

Correction – if the chaos was guaranteed to only bring good things then I am all down with that, but I quaver when it comes to the uncertainty of the horrible. I don't think it is entirely unreasonable to want to feel that you have some measure of control in an essentially unpredictable world. This has made me irritatingly sensible.

I was the eighteen-year-old at the pub too scared to have a beer because I didn't know what it would do to me and surely someone should be sober in case we were invaded or a tsunami hit and we needed a non-pissed person to point out the best way to higher ground. While others stood around coolly with their schooners, fag in the other hand, I slurped my pre-mix Coke and tried not to breathe in their passive smoke – cancer, gum disease, et cetera.

I have never bungee jumped, won't ever skydive and am overly liberal with hand sanitiser; I will rub it places not specified on the bottle (not there!). I will only use a public bathroom if there is enough left on the toilet roll to thoroughly paper the seat first. I do not take pleasure in ducking under waves, am rendered insensible by the hint of an undertow, cannot fathom those who cave dive.

When friends started to go to raves and take pills I dithered on the outer, convinced I would be the cautionary tale if I followed suit. Raves are not fun if you are sober. The music doofed and bleeped and the lights gave me a brain ache, and it was super boring; I was lurking by the exit before midnight. Okay, before ten.

While my nanna sensibilities were probably happy news to Mum's ears and, to be fair, shouldn't be cause for ridicule – we're not all designed to be super cool and laissez-faire with our personal safety or hygiene – the things not so easily controlled, the ephemeral, the unpredictable, were fodder for imaginatively lateral safety behaviour.

Anxiety isn't terribly sophisticated. Looking for patterns, it tells me that the reason I am safe, the reason everyone I know is alive and I haven't suffered any great catastrophes (touch wood!!) is because of entirely removed behaviours or objects. I find it impossible to throw away anything I have attached even the slightest sentimental meaning to. I have a drawer full of birthday cards given to me by various friends and relatives over the years that I am unable to throw away because what if the universe sees how callously I deal with something given to me and then decides to kill that person or strike them down with a terrible disease to teach me a lesson?

This is not sophisticated thinking. This is five-year-old thinking. But it is all the more durable for its illogicalities.

I link the status quo – my current wellbeing and lack-of-being-dead – with whatever I have been doing until now. I link it to the house I am living in, my hyper-vigilance, even a stupid pair of shoes that I don't want to get rid of for fear that horrible things will happen, that the shoes are the reason everything is all right. None of this is happening consciously and, when I realise I am doing it, it is easy to see how stupid this way of thinking is. But it festers away under the surface, gnawing at my gut when it comes time to pack a suitcase, leaping into my chest and burrowing into my brain when I have to move house, terrified I am tempting fate and that everything is about to end.

My magical thinking – believing that unlinked objects or actions might be able to influence the unfolding of events – doesn't just stop at the things I do or keep. I attribute meaning to every anxious twinge, every nervous gut, thinking it means imminent doom.

Every. Single. Time.

The fact that I seem to be far worse than a normal person at predicting the outcome of anything – I would go so far as guessing that I am worse than 95 per cent of the population – in no way lessens my conviction that *this time* my anxiety might be right and that I should ignore its warnings at my own peril.

Every time I was broken up with, even if I had clocked the warning signs, I was completely bamboozled. When my eldest son got chicken pox as a baby, and even with my extreme health paranoia, I thought it was mosquito bites until he developed a fever and my husband called the doctor.

I wonder if the reason I attribute such meaning to the sick turn of my stomach or my jittery heart or the nonsensical scary thoughts that run through my head is because I have such a hard time remembering them when they have passed.

Every time I have anxiety, the fear feels entirely real, entirely new. Even if it was never real before, even if I have panicked about this exact thing a thousand times, even if all those other times my fears were proved wrong, this time they might be right. I'm not entirely stupid – I know I have anxiety and have felt some version of this before, often this *exact* version – but the specifics are lost to the terror of the moment. When I am anxious, those fears feel important because they crowd out everything else – rational thought, objectivity, and even the ability to remember clearly what is happening in my body and mind, which renders future reflection a little tricky. I forget I've felt this exact feeling a bazillion times before and can only surmise that the bad feelings must mean that something awful is about to happen. It's only when others remind me that I was behaving exactly the same way just two hours earlier that I remember I've been here before.

I wonder if, in the manner of many crappy brain or emotional issues, my body's mode of protection – this weird anxiety amnesia – is actually making things worse? Superstitious thinking, while possibly a valid way to operate if you have no education or live in the Dark Ages, is an entirely pointless way to try to exert control, both then and now. It definitely didn't do many favours for all the women executed as witches in Salem in the 1600s.

Psychologically speaking, superstition refers to a set of behaviours that the person enacting them believes will influence unrelated events. Think of the young executive who will only deliver a big presentation if he is wearing his lucky underwear; the frequent flyer who will only sit in a certain row for fear the plane will crash otherwise; the me who thinks that keeping every picture my son draws, especially the crap ones, will protect him from disaster.

This is not just a human trait. It seems many creatures are designed to see patterns, even in the random, on the off chance that it may confer some kind of advantage or keep them safe. That they have control.

In his famous experiment, behavioural psychologist BF Skinner stuck some hungry pigeons in a cage and fed them at regular intervals, with no reference at all to the birds' behaviour, from an automated feeder. He found that the birds associated the arrival of food with whatever random behaviour they were exhibiting at the time and they continued to perform that in the hope it would bring them more food.[1] There's a lame joke to be made here about them being 'bird brained' but I'm worried about how that will reflect on me, both comically and because I do the same stupid shit.

A 1975 experiment demonstrated how the 'illusion of control' made people dramatically and irrationally overestimate the possibility they would succeed if they felt they had some measure of control, even if the outcomes were random.[2]

The best way to deal with a superstition is to challenge it. To think about it objectively, empirically. If forced to think about the connection between a birthday card and my husband's safety, it is readily apparent that this is mental. The ludicrousness of the belief can help with its dismantling. Laugh at yourself.

Then take small steps to dissolve the connection. Sure, you might not want to leap straight into a vital meeting without your lucky tie, but you might consider leaving it behind for something less important.

When I am having an episode, when the anxiety has passed manageable limits and my brain starts to look for the source of the danger, I will see meaning and import everywhere. If I flip open a magazine and it lands on a story about diabetes, I fear that is the universe trying to tell me that I am sick, that it's trying to give me signals while cursing me.

My brain means well – it's trying to keep me safe – but it honestly doesn't have any idea how to judge what is effective and what is fanciful.

Magical thinking – as it is sometimes known – is, to an extent, ubiquitous. We've all crossed our fingers for luck or knocked on wood to avoid jinxing ourselves because it makes us feel like we have some influence over things that are beyond our control.

While OCD and general anxiety are different disorders, they can sometimes present with similar thought patterns and behaviours. In an attempt to exert control and keep themselves safe, some anxious people or those with OCD will engage in behaviours that make no logical sense but will reduce the person's anxiety. Think of the woman who fills her house with possessions, even rusted soup cans or countless cats, because to get rid of anything would be to invite disaster.

Magical thinking refers to someone's belief that their thoughts or rituals can have distant physical and mental effects. The problem is that the more you indulge in this kind of thinking or play out these behaviours, the more they will be reinforced.

People with GAD will often describe themselves as having always worried, as the nervous child, the anxious teen. They might not even be able to say why they are worried or what caused it, just that they feel that something is not right.

16

Generalised anxiety disorder

Just the passage of time, if I think about it too much, can start to freak me out.

When I am feeling especially maudlin and nervy, I am plagued by the inexorable creep of my life toward something terrible – because every day that something bad doesn't happen is still one day closer to the day that something bad will happen (which is just about the most depressing sentence ever written). If you look at it that way, generalised anxiety disorder makes perfect sense! Of course I am freaking out! Today could be the day that everything changes for the worse and I don't know why but perhaps, just perhaps, if I think about all of those terrible things enough, if I pre-live them enough in my brain, I will somehow take the sting off them when they occur.

Of course, it makes way more sense to look at this as the ridiculously skewed logic that it is – there is no sense in forcing yourself to live through bad things twice (not only was it shit when I imagined getting cancer but it would be really bad if it happened).

Still, these hints of rationality don't stop my brain's slide into the worry and what-ifs.

Generalised Anxiety Disorder, or GAD, like all disorders, doesn't speak to the mere presence of anxiety. Almost everybody feels anxious sometimes – it is protective, even beneficial if felt in appropriate circumstances, when it makes you alert, sharpens your focus.

If you have GAD, however, you will feel anxious and worried most of the time, even when nothing stressful is happening, and it will affect the way you live your life. The worry can be about anything – health, work, love, kids, money – even if there is no real reason to be concerned. And there is the constant feeling of dread, that something very bad is about to happen.

Around 2.7 per cent of the Australian population will experience GAD each year, and it seems to affect women more than men.[1] People with GAD will often describe themselves as having always worried, as the nervous child, the anxious teen. They might not even be able to say why they are worried or what caused it, just that they feel that something is not right.

According to many therapists, CBT is the best way to

treat GAD, the techniques employed during treatment best address the thoughts and behaviours feeding the fear.

People with GAD have been shown to have significantly higher levels of avoidance (that old chestnut again) and distress about emotions than people without GAD. Intolerance of uncertainty is proposed as a defining feature of GAD, as is extreme worry.

It has also been suggested that worry is adopted by people with GAD as they see it as a way of helping them prepare for the uncertain things in life, or to superstitiously avoid future catastrophic events.[2]

This perfectly explains my own GAD. That in some way it protects me, keeps me hypervigilant to threats and practised in managing future terrible pain. I still have to work to challenge these thoughts when they creep back through the cracks that life can sometimes create.

Other Stories

M is an older woman with apple cheeks and twinkly eyes. She always looks out for me, is there to offer a sweet word of encouragement or an offer of help.

I had a panic attack coming back from New Zealand. It was awful. I had skolled champagne in preparation for getting on the plane because I hate flying, but to no avail. How was I to know the bloody plane ride back shoots up in the sky like a rocket! It was petrifying. How do I know I was anxious? Fear, sweating, feeling hot, wanting to get off the plane and not feeling in control, to name a few emotions. The woman next to me was stroking my hand and I didn't care. She was talking to me and asked to spray some lavender or something on my hand. So I began breathing it in deeply and focusing on breathing to get my mind off this awful feeling until the plane was not shooting upwards. It felt like forever but it was probably only a few minutes. And my husband turned around and said, 'WHAT did you do that for?' I think he was glad he was sitting in the aisle away from me. I am sure people around me thought I was nuts but I didn't care.

The last time I had a panic attack or anxiety attack was maybe eight years ago while Christmas shopping. I was feeling fine but I couldn't get a park and was driving around and around in the car park and I remember thinking, *Gosh, I am going to forget where I parked.* I did the shopping, went to the car, could not remember where it was. I broke out in a cold sweat, couldn't think clearly, could not remember where the car was, thought I wouldn't be able to get out. I stopped and sat on something and did some deep breathing before starting at the bottom and walking around to find it.

I think panic attacks and anxiety are hereditary. My mother has anxiety issues but won't acknowledge this. I try to plan things so I don't have a mild, brief panic attack. I knew someone who went to a psychologist to deal with anxiety. She confessed to me and I couldn't believe someone assertive and in control felt like that.

I've met so many people who seem to be confident and in charge of their lives who turn out to have anxiety. Long ago I stopped believing that there's a 'type' for anxious people. We are everywhere.

My first panic attack. And it was so
dreadful that, for years, I couldn't
imagine living a happy life, any life,
when I knew another such attack could
happen at any time.

17

Panic disorder and agoraphobia

I hadn't been to the gym, done any exercise in fact, for at least a year.

Living in London in my early twenties, I was more interested in drinking moderately (I felt quite safe having one beer, two on a big night, by this stage) and trying desperately to get a record deal by auditioning badly every couple of months.

The low point – although there were several contenders – was auditioning for a manufactured girl band I found advertised in *Stage*.

As the band was being put together by Stock and Aitken (Waterman had moved on to greener pastures by this stage), even just waiting in their foyer, surrounded by gold records awarded to Rick Astley and Kylie Minogue, I felt like I had made it.

Surprisingly I aced the singing part, belting a sub-par version of 'I Wanna Dance With Somebody'. Called back for the second round, assuming it would be some cursory singing and then a lot of deal signing and a limo ride home, I was thrown into immediate self-conscious meltdown when I walked into the room and realised I had to dance.

I do not dance.

In fact, I don't understand how anyone feels normal or comfortable dancing. I feel like an enormous beige octopus, boneless arms and legs flailing chaotically, without anything that even remotely resembles rhythm. Like a wobbly custard leaking bits all over the floor while trying to look cool and together, like one of those perfect fondant cake things instead.

Back in the studio and the girls already in the band – bronzed, blond, large-of-boob – began a complicated and contortionistic routine I knew I had absolutely no hope of doing, couldn't even remember anyway, and as they danced on my stomach hollowed out and I knew I was screwed.

I went through with it, waited for them to start the track again and threw myself around, cheeks flaming, while the others watched in complete silence. I think it was so bad that they didn't even feel comfortable laughing at me. When it was all over, when the track ended but nobody went to turn it off and the buzz at the end of the cassette went on and on, the choreographer gave me a kindly half-smile and shook her head.

Even as I closed the door there was nothing but silence from within.

After a few months off to recover my dignity (still looking) I found an ad for a new band, something equally inappropriate. But months of sensible drinking and not-so-sensible bacon-sandwich-gorging had meant I even struggled to walk up the nine stained stairs to our flat.

So to the gym I went. It wasn't a terribly intimidating gym, as far as gyms go: no grunting men in short-shorts hogging the mirror, no perky personal trainers in Lycra, so I was free to find a treadmill and shuffle-run to my heart's content. Or for about ten minutes.

But on my third or fourth visit and buoyed by new-fitness-regimen arrogance, there was a previously unseen hot girl already running on my preferred running machine. Her hair swung glossily; she sheened, didn't sweat, and I knew I had to beat her or die trying.

Reduced to using the treadmill sandwiched between her and the big window, and dowdy in my too-hot trackies and curry-stained T-shirt, I began.

It felt like all of my disappointments, all of my frustrations, all of my homesickness, poured into my legs and I ran like the clappers, feet blurring, machine set to an unreal 9 km per hour, wobbly arms shimmying by my sides, breath chafing my throat, eyes blurring. I had to beat her, had to keep going, couldn't slow or quit until she did first. If I could just beat her I would be picked at an audition, get a job that paid more than four pounds an hour, be confident, wise, sexually irresistible, less squid-like at dancing.

I couldn't guarantee which song would be thrown at me, whether I would get enough shifts at the bar to pay my rent or be able to stop my boyfriend from disappearing with the ginger waitress from New Zealand, but I made a deal with the universe that if I could just beat this girl, this time, this day, that the universe would allow only good things to happen. And I did.

She slowed her machine, then stopped, stepped off calmly and dabbed her brow with her clean white towel. As soon as she was around the corner I slammed on the emergency stop button, gripping exhaustedly to the hand rails as the belt juddered to a halt.

Heaving great breaths, I wobbly-stepped off the machine, heading for a cup of water at the fountain. Reaching for the plastic cup, everything lurched sideways and I felt like I was going to vomit and faint. I had never fainted before.

My first panic attack. And it was so dreadful that, for years, I couldn't imagine living a happy life, any life, when I knew another such attack could happen at any time.

My stomach yawed, the bottom dropping away into infinity. A normal person might have sat down, gone to the toilet to splash some water on her face, asked for help, but the thought of someone noticing was as bad as what was happening to me.

The thought that someone might feel sorry for me, or think something terrible was happening and call an ambulance, or be disgusted by my sweat and shaking, was more than I could bear. I was so scared of dying, and someone seeing, being witness to my debasement, that I would rather have died.

That is the evil of anxiety: you are so scared of dying that you think you would rather die than continue to feel the fear. It is ridiculous. Contrary. Perverse. Sadistic. And this first panic attack was triggered by a random confluence of all the things I was most afraid of – that I was losing control, that I was going to vomit in public, that someone would see and be disgusted by me, that I must have a terrible illness to have such bad symptoms.

My heart was thundering; I don't think I had ever felt it beat so fiercely. I was having a heart attack, an asthma attack, an aneurysm. Heat flooded my face, my stomach heaved but I swallowed it down. Everything felt sharp and blurry.

If I collapsed on that floor my life wouldn't be worth living. The thought of a fuss being made forced my feet to the door; my hand swung it open and I rounded the corner and lowered myself to the cement where no one could see.

I didn't, couldn't, make the connection between the anxiety I had felt all my life with this thing – this overwhelming, all-consuming, thing. I was sure I was dying.

I wouldn't make the connection between anxiety and the panic attacks for years, until I went home to Australia. But at this moment, down the sunny side of the gym, I felt all the fear I had felt years ago when I saw the drowning hole. Except this time I couldn't see the cause of my terror, didn't have anything to hang the fear on, nothing concrete to dread.

So it consumed me.

My heart eventually slowed; my vision widened; I began to notice the cars parked on the street, the sound of the people going in and out of the swinging door into the gym. I pulled myself to my feet and walked, ever so slowly, home.

I didn't tell Andy, or anyone, what had happened. I wanted to push it to some forgotten corner of my mind, although the shakiness lasted for days. And I feared it happening again.

As I lay awake that night, I desperately sought a rational reason, something that could have maybe caused this bizarre episode. I knew I was unfit but I thought that might have just made me breathe quickly, made me feel tired.

Then I knew it: I was hot. Too hot. I remembered Mum telling me that I had had a convulsion as a baby because I got too hot – conveniently forgetting that it was only once, childhood febrile convulsions are common, and it never happened again – and realised I must have some in-born sensitivity to heat. I had to be very careful from then on to never get too hot because if I did, I might die. The only reason I could have felt so infinitely bad at the gym was because I was so close to death.

•

Panic attacks are terrifying, especially when you are experiencing them for the first time, which is why so many people end up in emergency rooms thinking they are having a heart attack and dying.

Like mine, a first panic attack may often be associated with a stressful episode, but gradually the attacks become dissociated and occur 'out of the blue'. They usually last for around ten minutes, although that can vary. Some people might have a couple a year, others several a day.

Recognised symptoms are a pounding heart, sweating, shaking, hot flushes or chills, dry mouth and shortness of breath, feeling of choking, chest pain, nausea, numbness, dizziness, light headedness, feeling detached from yourself, and an intense fear of losing control, going crazy, dying.

Even though it can feel like you are the only person going through it at the time – I certainly couldn't fathom that something so vile could be a common experience – panic disorder is a relatively common problem: one UK study found that the lifetime prevalence, with or without agoraphobia, is about 1.70 per cent.[1] Beyond Blue reports up to 40 per cent of the Australian population will experience a panic attack in their life.[2] Some studies of patients presenting to emergency departments found that up to a quarter satisfied criteria for panic disorder.[3]

Panic disorder has also been associated with medical conditions like migraines, irritable bowel disorder and joint hypermobility, but more of that later.

Up to 40 per cent of people with panic disorder will also meet the criteria for agoraphobia.[4] Although a literal definition of agoraphobia is fear of open spaces, the clinical definition is closer to a fear of those places associated with panic attacks where escape is tricky, which leads to avoidance behaviours. The prominent feature of agoraphobia is avoidance of those situations where you are afraid a panic attack will happen, but this can become so broad that some people just stop leaving the perceived safety of their homes.

When I was in the absolute depths of panic disorder and agoraphobia, I could not conceive of ever again being able to live a life not overrun by panic attacks, ruined by them. I believed that now I knew feeling like that was possible, every day would be marred by them – if not by a panic attack then by the fear of having one. I wanted to go to sleep and not wake up until they were gone forever.

The sneaky thing about agoraphobia is that the panic will still eventually find you, no matter where you hide. My fear of dying from getting too hot was, by this stage, becoming so intense and illogical that a panic attack would be triggered if I saw someone who looked like they were feeling hot on the TV, like the time in San Diego when watching an ultramarathon on TV.

•

One of the best ways to recover from panic disorder and agoraphobia is to learn that the things you feel when in the grip of an attack, while extremely unpleasant, will not hurt you.

Once you've had one panic attack, just the fear of having another one, or going somewhere you have had one before, can be a trigger. When you are calm it is easier to recognise that the symptoms are dreadful but not intrinsically dangerous; this can all fly out the window, however, when you are in the middle of a panic attack. Because the bodily symptoms are so overwhelming it can be hard to think about anything except for them. Then the fear created by the feelings can worsen the symptoms as the body thinks it is in more danger – and round it goes.

A good place to start is to recall what you were thinking or feeling before and during an attack and write it down. Maybe even write down what you believe is going to happen to you during an attack. Do this at a time when you are *not* feeling panicky.

Then you challenge.

All the absolutes – *I'm dying, I'm going crazy, I can't cope* – are not actual facts, just skewed beliefs. Think of all the panic attacks you have survived before without losing your mind or toppling over dead or dropping down screaming in the middle of a shopping centre. Thinking the worst – catastrophising

– makes the panic worse. But setting up some rational, helpful self-talk can make things better. Instead of 'I'm dying' you might say, 'This sucks but I've survived all of the others and I'll be all right again this time'.

Exposure therapy aims to get phobic or panicky people back doing the things they have avoided through the fear that another panic attack would be triggered. To get them living their lives again.

Using my own sorry experience as an example, I avoided going out to see friends, as I was scared of being sick and having a panic attack in public, and this snowballed to the point where I just didn't leave the house at all. Unfun for everyone. But if someone had told me to face my fear and forced me to go straight to a massive outdoor concert in the middle of a summer's day, I might have felt too overwhelmed by the idea to even get out of the car and the avoidance would have been reinforced even more.

Better to start small. Go for a short walk to the end of the road with a friend. When you accomplish that, even if you feel terrified and shit, your confidence gets a boost and your anxiety takes a hit. Then gradually increase the distance.

The first time I left the house to do more than sit in the car while my mum shopped was to see a friend. She wanted to go to a pub but I suggested a park. I was grossly uncomfortable, my heart pumped alarmingly and I hardly said a word, but thankfully my kind friend pretended not to notice. I left after thirty minutes, but I had showed myself that I could do it. I could sit with the vile feelings and not die or make a fool of myself or collapse. And next time the feelings of panic were less. And less. And less.

If you're not sure how best to set these kinds of goals, or you just don't know how or when to start, speak to a psychologist.

Learning to breathe slowly is a really important technique when you are having a panic attack, even though you might feel like you want to breathe faster because you feel like you're not getting enough air.

Breathing too quickly can cause a lot of the symptoms associated with panic attacks, so if you can calm your breathing you can also calm the symptoms. This is another thing to practise when you are calm so it comes more readily and easily in times of panic. You can even test this out for yourself by overbreathing when you are not anxious to see how it triggers those physical sensations.

The person trapped in a cycle of panic attacks is a frightened person indeed. Imagine knowing that, at any moment and mostly without warning, you could be engulfed, smothered, drowned by the knowledge that you are dying, that your body is reacting so fiercely to the threat that it could only be true; you feel like your heart will explode, you will soil yourself, faint, throw up, go mad, and it is worse around people and when the attacks first start, before you know what they are and can work to understand and beat them, you will feel like you are dying and, sometimes, the attacks will be so bad you would welcome it.

Go gently with that person. They have stared into the abyss.

18

Nervous breakdown

For me, it felt like the deepest, heaviest, bleakest exhaustion. And sadness, utter sadness.

They don't tend to call it a nervous breakdown these days – it's a 'mental health crisis' – but nervous breakdown perfectly describes how I was feeling when I moved back in with my parents after the breakup with Andy. For so long I had been running with all of my nerves exposed, my body thrumming with adrenaline, muscles taut, heart aching, that it felt as though my body just gave up everything else, gave up anything that wasn't sadness or anxiety.

I felt thick with grief, like I was made of wet sand, and at the same time humming with nervousness, like I was composed of both electricity and sludge.

Mornings were the worst. I slept as long as possible – ten, twelve, fourteen hours – hoping to miss the morning entirely. When I finally woke I would have a moment of normal, as if everything was okay, and then it would come, the knowledge I had to make it through another day, all the hours I had to survive until I could go back to sleep, and the anxiety would knife through my chest with a sharp blade. *Another day, another day, another day.* Another day when bad things could happen.

I didn't care that my hair was greasy and matted. Didn't care that spring had arrived and the willow was tapping its new leaves against the roof.

Mum brought food to my door, tried to tempt me with my favourite things and I rejected them all and took pleasure in the worry on her face because it was a knife of guilt in my gut and I deserved it.

One night, after another day of anxiety and crying and feeling so utterly desperate and hopeless, Dad came to my door. Mum was sitting at the foot of my bed for the umpteenth night in a row, patting my leg, and I had my face buried in my pillow. When Dad appeared I stopped crying and peered up with one eye. I was too embarrassed to sob publicly, retained a tiny bit of self-respect, even then, and didn't want Dad to look at me like I was hopeless even though I would have believed him.

He stood there for a few moments, then took a step into the room. He was never one to say much about how he felt – say anything, in fact.

'I know a little how you feel,' he said. 'I was very scared of your grandfather – my Dad – when I was growing up. When he would come into the room I would wet myself from fear.'

I knew he must have been worried about me then; I can't imagine anything else that would have driven him to share something so exposing and, for a moment, I wanted desperately to get better, just so he would be proud and know that revelation had meant something. But it was just too hard.

Friends rang – the few who knew somehow that I had come home – and I would shuffle down the hall to the phone, cradle the receiver to my face and cry and cry and hang up. I told Mum to tell them I was busy when they rang back.

If I could have slept until I felt better I would have, no matter how long it took. If I was never going to feel better I wanted to sleep forever.

Books and web pages describe a 'nervous breakdown' in similar ways: you will stop being able to function in normal day-to-day life, and normal demands or activities become physically and emotionally overwhelming. A nervous breakdown includes seemingly prosaic problems like feeling isolated, being unable to concentrate and feeling moody, to truly scary things like depersonalisation (when you feel detached from reality), hallucinations and thoughts of self-harm.

It is essential to make an appointment with your doctor if you think you might be having a nervous breakdown, but it would have been easier to sprout wings and fly to Nepal than to have taken myself to a doctor when I was in this place.

I needed others to step in, wanted others to fix me because I didn't even know who I was any more, let alone being capable of figuring out how to get back to who I had been.

I stopped eating.

Always thin, I got smaller and smaller, wished myself away. This wasn't anorexia. I just didn't want food, didn't see the point. To eat and sleep and then wake up and do it again – why?

Mum cajoled, begged, bullied, to try to get me to eat. Finally she dragged me to a new doctor who took one look and ordered me onto the scales.

Forty-three kilograms.

He said if I didn't start eating he would be forced to have me sectioned – that is, I would be admitted to a psychiatric hospital whether I wanted to be or not.

Mum thinks this is the moment things started to get better and I can only believe her, as I don't remember that visit to the doctor, nor do I remember being told I had to eat. I do remember, though, that I started eating again and I cried the whole time – a mixture of fear of being sick and despair that moving on, getting better, would mean that the part of my life that Andy had been a part of, no matter how painful, was really over.

They say your first love is always a tough one to get over, even if it isn't the realest love you will ever have, or the truest. Even when the best is waiting just around the corner. I want to go back in time and touch that girl on the shoulder and whisper into her ear, 'This is not the one for you'.

I agreed to try an anti-anxiety medication. When that one did bugger-all I tried another and we found something that took the edge off the panic. For the first time in months and months I felt something of myself come back. It's not the same for everyone, I am sure, and I hated the thought of being medicated, as I didn't want to live a life I didn't think would be authentic. It was ridiculous that I would rather continue to feel shit than feel better because medication had stopped my brain from wanting to abandon ship.

I usually hate an uplifting quote, find them facile, even offensive, so when people – who I guess were trying to help in my darkest hours – recited stupid platitudes like 'god/ the universe/the great-unicorn-in-the-sky never gives you more than you can handle', I wanted to scream. People get more than they can handle all the time. People harm themselves because they have been given more than they can handle. Stupid statements like this make people feel bad for not coping and devalue the pain they are feeling, the trouble they are in. And if people feel like they are failing because they are not coping, they are not going to want to ask for help for fear of looking weak. I didn't want to ask for help even though I desperately, desperately needed it.

Don't say that kind of thing.

And if you are suffering and someone does say that kind of thing, ignore them. If you have been given more than you can handle, accept help, seek help. Family, friends, professionals: these people can shoulder the load when you are crumbling. There is no shame in not being able to do it alone.

There was, however, one quote that did help during this time, that I found randomly in a magazine in the crammed shelves near my bed; it made me feel like even the damaged ones might be good for something: 'There is a crack in everything. That's how the light gets in.'

One warm night, while I was still living with Mum and Dad but I wasn't just a shadow any more, there was a quiet tap at my bedroom door.

Mum poked her head around, a small-teeth smile.

'Can I come in?'

'No, bugger off.'

She gave a small laugh and came in. Held out a small parcel wrapped in tissue paper.

'This is for you.'

Mum has always been good at craft. Every year she made us a present, on top of the mountains of stuff she and Dad would buy. One year she made me a beautiful dollhouse, with electric lights that really worked and an old-fashioned husband and wife and a baby in a carriage. I was keener on the horse that pulled a wagon of barrels in the tiny street out front but the pram was good for transporting the dolls into the house so the mum and dad could have some home-tapped beer.

Mum made Ben an enormous train set, bigger than our dining table, with multiple tracks that went through tiny towns, over mountains, past work sites and hedged lanes. We carefully jimmied the glued-down people and cars off, one by one, so we could make new towns under the couch.

Another year she made us life-size dolls and because mine was slightly bigger than Ben's, I could use it to semi-smother him and stifle his cries when I was beating him up.

My school-play costumes were always better than the other kids' and were probably most of the reason why I always got the starring role (the other being that I was a bossy cow, even to the teachers). For all my childhood quirks and obsessions, stage fright was not something I was afflicted with then, even when things went wrong. I remember starring in a play in Year Three or Four, something to do with Japan, and my mum had made me a fabulous satin kimono that trailed on the floor behind me and gathered at my waist with a bright pink obi. Midway through our first performance – in front of the terrifying Year Sevens, no less – I couldn't work out how to open the fake door that had been fashioned by some disinterested Year Twos (and was covered in suspicious fingerprints). So I just hoicked the trailing satin over my hips and clambered over the top. Everyone laughed but I just swished my kimono a bit and watched with glee as the other little girls' faces reddened in furious envy.

Mum held market stalls, piled with jams and white Christmas; sold patchwork quilts to a boutique in the hills; was famous for the jumpers she knitted for relatives, even though it would often take her years to finish one.

Grandpa, right to the end, would often wear a jumper Mum had knitted for him as a teen. It was a burnt-orange colour and had moth holes in the chest and sleeves. He wore it under his professor's jacket on cold days.

Mum sat next to me on the bed as I tore off the paper.

Inside were two newborn-baby shoes. Mum had covered them in red sequins, stitched on one by one, and then tied them together with a red ribbon.

I looked at her with a raised eyebrow.

'Now you're better I wanted to make these to remind you if you ever feel bad again,' Mum said. 'It's from *The Wizard of Oz*, at the end when Dorothy thinks she can't make it back home, back to who she was.

'The Good Witch points at her shoes, tells her to click them together three times, to say, "There's no place like home."

'She tells her, and remember this, "You've always had the power, my dear, you just had to learn it for yourself."'

Those shoes, which remind me of those days when the light began to creep back in through the cracks, have followed me interstate and overseas and now sit in the bottom drawer of the chest beside my bed. They've lost more than a few sequins along the way, and the ribbon fell off years ago. But I treasure them. They are love.

Other Stories

I met G through my husband and she was one of the first to buy me a beer when I moved to Queensland and to make me feel like less of a friendless loser.

My anxiety leads to insomnia. And then the anxiety gets worse. It can lead to constipation, even. I really have to watch myself that I relax in the evening, don't work at night, exercise and eat well. I've worked out a few coping mechanisms over the years, like switching off from my daily life after 10 p.m., doing yoga and Crossfit or running.

The stuff that goes through my thoughts when I'm in the grip of it range from things like regretting something I should have said to someone twelve years ago, to what will I do when my cat dies (actually I have a few issues around dead pets), if I don't get home right now my cat will be run over by a car, and also turning into my street and expecting to see my cat run over.

I usually recognise it for what it is now and just try to breathe or talk myself out of it. If it's late at night I might switch my light on and read a chapter of something fictional. It's really only mild though and has never stopped me from leading a full life – perhaps not always realised my full potential – but I'm much better at it now.

19

Recovery

When the worst of the panic subsided, when the meds kicked in and I could stomach toast and sit in the lounge room without dissolving, Mum got me to a psychologist.

It took some doing.

For anxiety treatments in general, you have to explore a bit to find the thing that works best for you. Same goes for the therapists themselves.

By this time it was summer and, although medication had taken the edge off my panic, I was still convinced that I would overheat and die in the sun.

The psychologist who eventually helped, although probably not for the reasons he thought, began counselling me over the phone when I was still too raw and easily panicked to leave the safety of the house.

When I finally made it to his rooms, in a sad '70s office block north of the city, he took me through the usual questions, asking about my mum and dad, I guess to work out what trauma they had inflicted upon me that might be an easy problem to address. Then he asked me about the anxiety and panic attacks. I blurted out the lot. The constant worry, the dread, the jitters and thudding heart and crook guts and shakes-faints-sweats. Told him that I had begun to believe very frightening things were true. That I didn't have any hope that I could live without the fear of another panic attack.

He looked at me, a tiny man with a tightly trimmed beard and wire-rimmed glasses, like a hipster Freud but with bad pants, and said, 'You poor thing, that sounds horrible.'

To have someone other than my family recognise the brutality of anxiety meant everything, that it wasn't in my head, that he believed I wasn't putting it on for attention, and that if he knew how bad this kind of thing could be maybe he also knew how to stop it.

Of course, nothing is that simple, nor that quick.

He knew I was afraid of heat so would take me for rides in his car, a fancy German thing with leather interior and seat warmers. I knew – or was eighty-five per cent positive – that he wasn't a murderer or sex pest so felt relatively relaxed (not having an internalised meltdown). As we drove he would sneakily, or so he thought, turn up the heating under my seat until it became a bit warm. I knew he was doing this and didn't have the heart to tell him I was wise to his game. He asked me how I felt and, not wanting to disappoint him, I would say, 'Oh, fine, all good', and he would twinkle with satisfaction and let me in on the seat-heater secret.

I knew he was hoping that exposing me to heat in a safe environment would help me overcome my phobia, and maybe it did to an extent, but I was never going to panic in his safe car. Not only was I with someone who was not going to let me die, but I could just take off my jumper or, worst-case scenario, he could drive me the 300 metres down the road to the enormous hospital. The problem I had was not in these controlled situations but outside in the wild. Who would help me when I was stuck outside in the middle of a brutal summer day with no water or shade, when my heart started to pump and I shook and felt like I was going to vomit, when I looked around for safety and there was nothing? Who would help me when I had to venture beyond my 'safety zones' and risk death? Who would carry a spray bottle of water and a bucket of ice for me at all times?

Yet the fear did subside; my heat phobia joined the drowning hole bit by bit, until all that remained was a damp spot on the floor. Just living saw it off. Edging my way into scary situations step by step. A two-minute walk in the hot sun, then later a stroll around the block. Meeting friends at the beach without a swimming costume so I couldn't just sit in the shallows.

I was eventually well enough to resume my life as a slightly-less-mental 25-year-old; I moved out of my parents' place and stopped seeing that psychologist. Because I didn't have a job and had spent any money left over from London on clothes that didn't fit me when I started eating again, Mum said she would help me out with rent until I found work.

My old friend Amy had a spot in her house in the city, a great room with a balcony that looked over the cigarette-strewn courtyard of the sobriety centre next door. They were a friendly lot, would wave and mumble hello as we wandered past in the mornings when I finally went back to university. Though they stretched the friendship a little when they started cutting off bits of our hose to siphon petrol from nearby cars to sniff. Amy and I wrote what we thought was a brilliant note from our fake detective-father, threatening arrest and prison for anyone caught stealing any more hose. So they stole my car instead.

I scored a job at a pub just down the road, started studying again. Life, from the outside, looked like pretty standard twenty-something fare.

A couple of years later, when the anxiety began to slither its way back into my veins, I saw another psych who lived in a hoarder's paradise in an affluent suburb near the city.

Totally normal and fancy-looking from the outside, inside the walls quivered with stacks of paper and sagging boxes. If I managed a quick glance down the hallway on the way to the therapy room I could see the part where he lived and this did not fill me with confidence. Nor did the man himself. He looked like a giant walking beanbag, dishevelled, clad in corduroy, and he did the office work as well as the therapy. Each session I would find him somewhere underneath the shifting papers, would pull out my wallet and pass over my bank card for his swiping machine, which sometimes worked but mostly didn't.

The picture on his business card showed him holding what looked like a crystal ball – I'm still not sure what that was. The therapy room was decorated with crooked posters about couples counselling, more towers of books, a sagging couch and African tribal totems.

Once there he would make me do strange things, like leap energetically to my feet while yelling, 'I FEEL GREAT!' Mostly I just felt embarrassed and stupid and anxious that he was secretly taking the piss out of me and I was too gullible to be able to tell.

At the end of each session he would take me through a guided meditation that he would simultaneously burn onto a CD scavenged from under one of the leaning piles of office detritus. I had to pay extra for these, although he did, thoughtfully, always ask me what colour I 'felt' like that day, before scribbling it on the cover.

One time his nose started bleeding and he didn't notice for almost five minutes. I knew it took this long as I timed it on the wall clock behind his head while shrinking in my chair, terrified he would snort his bloody nose germs all over me but too freaked out to tell him as I didn't want to make him feel embarrassed. He finally noticed when the blood dripped onto his leg and he shuffled to the back of the house, muttering about tissues and Band-aids. He was gone for quite a while. When he came back he told me we were out of time.

Seeing a doctor for anxiety, especially if it is the first time, can be embarrassing and scary. I remember being terrified I would either be immediately locked away in a padded room or laughed out of the surgery (and I wasn't sure what would be worse). And it is entirely possible the first doctor or therapist you see won't be the right one for you. Perseverance is vital. No matter how many nose-bleeding, paper-hoarding, rabbit-breeding (a *whole* other story) professionals you see, it is worth it to push through until you find the right person for you. It can really make all the difference to your recovery.

By making my way through a wide spectrum of professionals over the years – from shonk to miracle-worker – I found that what worked for me when my panic attacks were still raw was a combination of medication and CBT.

Today, when my anxiety is far, far milder and panic attacks few and far between, I have found other things that work, combinations that make me feel strong. But I feel stronger knowing I have these other things ready if I fall.

20

CBT and ACT and MBCT

The exact application of cognitive behavioural therapy differs between disorders but the fundamentals remain true.

Very basically, CBT is employed to help someone with anxiety alter their emotional distress and dysfunctional behaviour. This is true of many therapies.

The 'cognitive' part of CBT proposes that the way we think about a situation affects how we react – that thinking irrationally about something can lead to unhealthy anxiety about it. So the C part of the therapy looks at identifying those thoughts and assumptions that create and maintain anxiety and then challenges them with logic and evidence. The anxious person then practises these new, healthier ways of thinking so as to solidify them.

It is very hard to think your way out of anxiety when you are in it, though, which is why CBT has the B bit.

The behavioural part targets avoidance because avoidance, in the long run – as I've already described in my own life – maintains and increases anxiety.

And the best way to get over avoidance? You guessed it: face the fear.

Prolonged exposure therapy will slowly but surely whittle away the connection the brain has made between a particular stimulus and danger. But if you are afraid of water, you can't just jump in the shallow end and immediately leap out and expect to be cured. The tough part of the therapy is that you have to be prepared to be 'with' the anxiety long enough for it to begin to reduce, so that the brain can learn that the feared consequence didn't happen and that some anxiety is tolerable and does eventually lessen.

There are different kinds of exposure therapy that are used, dependent on the kind of anxiety being experienced. For example, if you have post-traumatic stress disorder after serving during war, a therapist might get you to remember the traumatic event until the brain stops reacting to it (because the memories aren't dangerous, even though they might be unpleasant).

Cognitive behavioural therapy has helped me get rid of particular phobias that were concrete – water and heat – because exposure was easy.

Acceptance and commitment therapy (ACT) is a more recent mindfulness-based behaviour therapy.

While CBT was helpful for those concrete phobias, the ACT way of approaching anxiety makes more sense to me than CBT in terms of health anxiety. I have to accept that there is sickness and uncertainty, that these are part of life.

Instead of focusing on symptom reduction (although proponents say symptom reduction will still be achieved), ACT aims to instil acceptance that life is inherently imperfect, and that sometimes there is pain but that a rich and meaningful life is the goal. It focuses very much on being 'in' the moment – being present. Anxiety is essentially future focused: the anxious mind fears the unknown, fears that what is to come could be bad; ACT teaches mindfulness to keep the patient in the here and now.

So the A stands for accepting that unwanted things and feelings will happen and they are out of our control, and the C bit stands for commitment towards living your life anyway.

I find it incredibly hard to be in the moment; it's something I have to practise and really work at, and I am lazy and hate practising and working. Being in the moment is all about letting thoughts come and go, observing them but not judging them, or trying to control them or place meaning on them. It's about engaging fully in whatever you are doing.

Mindfulness-based cognitive therapy (MBCT) does not seek the eradication of unwanted or horrible thoughts, rather the acceptance of them and being able to decide what merits your attention, because everybody has unwanted thoughts and feelings.

Hold the damn phone. Is this true?

Does *everybody* really have unwanted thoughts and feelings – even the people who are not anxious all the time? I honestly thought we were few and far between. And, if this is true, how do these people not keel over from anxiety if they are also thinking about the gruesome ways their kids might die?

By being in the moment. By seeing thoughts as just that, thoughts, moments in their heads, and of no more import than a show on the television. And by being kind to themselves, letting go of judgement. Taking an attitude of compassion instead of fear.

21

Marriage

The first time I saw my husband he had a ponytail and a missing tooth and a twinkle in his eye.

He categorically denies my memory of our first conversation and is resolute that he would never say anything quite so lame. But I swear this is true.

It was his first day working at the bar I was managing – terribly, as I spent more time hiding downstairs playing Solitaire on the computer and eating masses of cheese paninis than doing any actual managing – and he was drawing chalk pictures of Vespas on the blackboards.

'So, what are you doing in London?' he asked.

Being cool and a total pro at flirting without showing off, I said, 'Just working here in between auditions, you know. I'm a singer, this is just something I do to make extra money.'

He grinned at me. 'I was in a musical once, at school,' he said, 'but I haven't met my leading lady yet.'

Bad pick-up lines, ponytails and questionable dental work aside, Josh showed me kindness when I needed it most.

I unravelled in London, slowly to start with, but inexorably. The tightly held corners of my life frayed and burst and my insides spilled out – the anxieties, the panic, everything I had worked so hard for so many years to keep secret was there for everyone to see.

Josh was only ever a friend there; I still thought Andy, in his ever-increasing distance, was the one for me.

Josh let me stay in his one-room bedsit when I was between flats. Let me bunk down on the floor in front of his telly, awkwardly, squashed. He let me sleep in his bed when I was tired and had a break at work, and he sat on the edge and let me talk and never tried anything, and smiled. He listened as I babbled and flirted and complained and big-noted, and he smiled and smiled and asked questions, and he felt comfortable to me, like home, even then.

Once back in Australia, when I was bereft, he would email and call to see how I was.

And when we finally found ourselves in the same place – to be honest, I had a friend who was staying in Brisbane and I had always wondered about Josh and figured, well, two birds, one stone, et cetera – I was a goner.

Josh comes from a big, close family: he is one of seven and is a twin, and his brother is so disturbingly similar, even though they swear they are not identical, that I once walked out of our room starkers because I thought it was Josh talking on the phone in the hallway. It was not Josh. But Josh has seen his sister-in-law in the nude in similar circumstances so I guess being a twin isn't completely without its merits.

In the beginning, when Josh was just learning about my anxiety, his family found it hard to understand exactly what the hell was going on with me. Outgoing and friendly one moment, in the next I would shut down, make my excuses and disappear to our room to try to head off a panic attack before it took over. As someone trying to get over panic attacks that were triggered by heat, moving to Queensland in the middle of summer probably wasn't the most sensible idea, and I spent much of those first months somewhere between panic and drunkenness.

Josh is the calmest of the calm: he wouldn't know a panic attack if it smacked him in the back of the head, although he tries his hardest to understand mine. His siblings, for the most part, share that calmness and I think they found my behaviour odd.

It was so hot in our house – which was mid-renovation and felt like a sweatbox inside – that Josh asked his brother, a sparkie, to install an air-conditioner in our room to try to help me find a place to feel calm. When his brother arrived to install it I was on the edge of a panic attack and lay on the couch with a wet cloth to try to stay calm while he sweated like crazy in our room. I'm sure he thought I was a complete cow – from the outside it probably looked like I was the laziest person known to man, especially as I still didn't have the words to explain panic attacks to others.

However, life went on. I was on medication, my panic attacks would lessen, I would go off the meds and enjoy months of feeling pretty good, of coping, then something would happen to trigger them – a change at work, summer, missing home – and I would spiral out of control and go back on them again to try to find some peace.

Josh proved a constant: the first person since Mum who I felt I could lean on who wouldn't be disgusted by my weakness, who didn't mind that I wasn't perfect, who was used to the vagaries of relationships and life. Coming from a big family, being a twin, I think this has made him able to bear stress well. He doesn't even flinch when I crack, just does the things that need to be done, steps up when I can't even stand, and loves me.

He also tells me I am being a dick if I try to manipulate him and likes to tell long stories about things I have no interest in. We can't go to the movies without him snoring, he fidgets through nice dinners because he gets bored with all the sitting. We have fights and yell nonsensical insults at each other but neither of us are painful silent-treatment types. He is unlike many in that he can say sorry (I am still learning), and he is my best friend.

We got married after our babies because we were young and sophisticated people of the world, or lazy, whatever, and the stress of organising a day that couldn't be escaped without drama – not because of my relationship, but for the fear of what I would do if someone got sick, if the boys got gastro, or flu, or broke an arm, and everything was called off – plagued me.

Putting so much expectation on one day felt like an invitation for disaster to me. Like letting the magical beings that control everything know that this one day was so important was tantamount to erecting a huge fluoro sign out the front of my house with SCREW YOU, UNIVERSE flashing on it in huge pink lights.

I fretted up until the day itself. Wanted to keep the kids away from everyone so they wouldn't catch anything, but Josh had organised a dozen family-and-friend events in the lead-up and the boys were in heaven running around with random kids and rellies, and what could I say?

On the day, though, because the planets aligned, because the universe smiled – or perhaps just because, after all this bloody time, my stupid brain absorbed a thing or two – I was in my wedding.

Really in it, the moment.

I didn't worry about the kids and Edward did vomit on himself for some unknown baby reason, Sam had a tantrum, it was hot, and I just felt happy.

And calm.

And like whatever happened wouldn't really matter, not in the big scheme of things.

Other Stories

P is married to my best male mate. She looks you square in the eye when she talks, speaks her mind, and doesn't seem to give two dicks what anyone else thinks about it. She has anxiety.

I have suffered from anxiety over the years, mostly because I'm a control freak and perfectionist. Mostly it's connected to my work because the jobs keep piling up and I can't be a slack teacher, I have to be a great one! I feel sick, tense, almost tingly all over, I have trouble sleeping, lose my appetite and become a snappy bitch. I am loving not working now!

I have felt moments of anxiety since having babies, maybe because I have three of them. I know a lot of that is sleep deprivation too.

I assume it's genetic. My brother suffered from anxiety and depression and took his own life last year. Sometimes it only lasts a few minutes, sometimes a few days. I used to worry a lot in my last relationship but my husband is such a calming influence on me. A few years ago I got sick and ended up being diagnosed with chronic fatigue but when the doctors didn't know what it was I was pretty freaked out and anxious. As soon as I had a reason, the anxiety settled. At the time I considered medication and if the doctor had said that the meds would have worked immediately I would have taken them, but he said it would take weeks and I just hoped I would relax and not worry.

Sometimes I can talk myself out of it, other times I just have to ride the waves. I am a massive talker if something bothers me, so I do mostly that to calm myself, and wine and chill-time helps.

I don't know if I will ever go back to teaching now that I know how nice it feels to not be stressed and anxious all the time.

Not everyone is in the position to give up their job to avoid feeling anxious – and, as my own experience and research shows, avoidance can be a dicey tactic anyway – but P's story shows us that sometimes making choices that lead to the life you would rather live can be as effective as other treatments. No job is worth feeling uncertain and anxious so much of the time.

Josh held our new baby, Sam, and the smile on his face was everything I wished I could feel. But I couldn't because that damned anxiety was back, licking its tongue at the bottom of my spine, whispering in my ear that I was trapped now, that I was dying.

22

Pregnancy

The work toilet was small and brown-tiled, set off the underground car park and only accessible by a key tied by a questionably greasy rope to an old wooden spoon.

Brooke and I squashed into the stall together to read the instructions on the test.

My period wasn't even late but I felt a bit odd – my belly felt dense, full – and I thought, in the manner of many bored twenty-something women, that grabbing a pregnancy test with a friend and then being able to laugh and get a wine afterwards when it came back negative would be an all right way to spend the afternoon.

I never wanted kids. I've never been clucky, never cooed over a tiny cousin or gazed wistfully at babies snoozing in pushers. I never babysat, hated holding friends' newborns, was annoyed by squealing kids in parks.

But there, on the test, was a something. Not a line. But, if you squinted, the very faintest blue something.

I showed Brooke.

'Um, I don't know, I don't think there is anything there,' she said.

'But what's that really faint bluish smudgey bit?'

'Oh. Maybe some pen?'

'Yeah. Shit. Probably.'

Back at my desk I knew. I felt my stomach drop, a hollowness, dread.

That afternoon after work I went to the doctor at the shopping centre down the hill from my house.

I told her that I had done a test and maybe there was something on there but probably not and, after all, I was kind of prone to anxiety and chances are I was being crazy but I thought I should come in and check.

Just in case.

She gave me another urine test, the same kind I had taken hours before.

She held it in her hand distractedly while she asked about work and when I had had my last pap smear.

She looked at the test almost as an afterthought.

'Congratulations, you are pregnant!' she announced. 'And, if the dates of your last period are correct, you are due on Boxing Day.'

She said other things, about vitamins and no more wine, but her voice blurred under the beating of my heart.

I walked back up the hill, fed the dog, sat on our old tattered couch, and willed the pregnancy to come undone.

When Josh got home I sobbed that I had been to a doctor and I was pregnant but couldn't be, didn't want to be. Standing in the doorway, he said all the things a good man is meant to say in situations like this.

'It's your decision. I'll do whatever you want to do.'

We went to a late-night doctor because I thought that maybe the other one had made a mistake, maybe the test was faulty. This doctor was grandfatherly, got me to take the same test yet again.

Pregnant.

Again the congratulations and the advice, recommendations for maternity hospitals and obstetricians.

I cried but I think he took my tears for those of happiness; he patted my back on the way out, telling me I would be a good mum.

But I knew, as soon as I knew there really was a baby, that I could not have it.

I asked Josh to make the phone calls that would lead to there being no more baby.

The patting doctor, sorry that he had mistaken my tears for joy, told Josh where we could go, that a threat to my mental health was sufficient cause to seek an abortion in Queensland, but that I would have to be the one to make arrangements so they knew I wasn't being coerced into doing something I didn't want to do.

A week later, and just five weeks into the pregnancy, we went to get the abortion.

I had imagined being faced with an angry horde that would wave pro-life banners in my face while yelling about my unborn child. Instead, the clinic was on a quiet street; its only difference to the homes around it was the intercom at the door and the locked gate.

I'd expected to be the oldest woman there. Thought I would be surrounded by po-faced teens in their school uniforms being consoled by cross mothers. But there was only one girl there. One woman came alone and stared at a magazine, quiet in her jeans and singlet. An older woman, grey-haired in glasses, sat with hands crossed in her lap and eyes closed. Another kissed her toddler daughter and husband goodbye at the door.

Because the pregnancy was so new, the doctor needed to do an internal ultrasound to make sure there was something there.

I don't know why but he angled the ultrasound screen to me and showed me the small circle, so small it didn't even have a noticeable heartbeat yet.

'See that – that blot?' he asked, voice thick with an accent I couldn't place.

'Yes.'

'That's your baby. It's one of the earliest I have seen here.'

It seemed cruel, pointing that out, but my guilt meant I felt I deserved it.

The nurse got me out of my clothes and into a gown, asked for the sanitary pad I had been told to bring for afterwards, and held my hand when I lay on the table waiting for them to put me under.

I am resolutely pro-choice and believe firmly in the right for a woman to have autonomy over her body. I think abortion should be easy to access, safe and affordable.

None of this, however, meant that I felt good about my decision. I felt horribly sad. But the anxiety was so immense: having control taken away from me, thinking about caring for a child I had never planned for and didn't want was too much. I could not wait to have my body back, to be rid of what felt like a terrorist, a parasite.

When I woke up after the procedure, as I sat in recovery with my cheese sandwich, when I got home and went for a walk to the oval with my dogs, I felt sad but, more than anything, I felt relief.

•

Whether it threw some kind of biological switch, whether I had just spent time thinking about babies for the first time in my life, whether I was noticing smiling mothers for the first time, whether it was brainwashing from years of Catholic school conditioning and guilt over the 'sacredness' of life, I now wanted a baby.

Towards the end of the year, when that first baby would have been born, we decided to pack up and move closer to my parents.

In typical-me fashion, I spent the first two weeks after we moved to Adelaide twisted in regret, certain I had made the wrong decision, that everything was about to go tits up, that tragedy and horror were about to befall us.

My new boss was terrifying, a looming moustache who would yell across the newsroom and make vague threats about what may befall the poor journo who didn't get a story over the line.

'You, YOU!' he would roar across the floor. 'There's going to be an Elisa-shaped hole in that window if you don't find out where Snoop Dogg is drinking tonight.'

I would nod with a shit-eating smile and bolt out to lurk outside Snoop Dogg's hotel in the hope one of his posse would stop and talk. (They always do.)

My plans for pregnancy progressed quickly, as I filled myself with beta-blockers and tried not to cry at my desk.

I got myself off all the anti-anxiety medication, even though my doctor had said that what I was taking was fine. Unconvinced, I didn't want to do anything that might hurt this baby. I stopped reading the true-crime books I usually read with relish, because I was paranoid my baby-to-be might absorb the evil.

Funny how the decision to create something changes entirely what you are willing, or not, to do for it.

It took me four months to get pregnant with my first son and in that time I convinced myself that I was being punished for the abortion, that I would never have a baby as the universe had deemed my uterus (and the rest of me) unfit for motherhood.

The third time my period came, in a fit of dramatic pique I threw myself down in front of the bookshelf and cried to an old-person radio station dedicated to 'Saturday Night Love Songs' because I knew I was destined to have lots of dogs and would end up like the lady who stares angry-wistfully at other people's children and offers them inappropriate lollies, like the old duck at the supermarket who tries to steal my kids now whenever I go to buy bread.

After three months of no baby, in an effort to exert some control over the seemingly uncontrollable, I went to see an acupuncturist who friends whispered about in awed voices.

Young, and looking like the guitarist in a cover band, he stuck needles in my face, abdomen, hands and feet, and chattered about his own baby daughter.

I thought it was all bollocks and I was pregnant by the end of that month.

•

Even off the anti-anxiety meds, going through pregnancy and hormonal as all get-out, I was the calmest I had been in years. (By the time I became accidentally pregnant with my second son I was firmly back on the happy pills; he is perfectly fine and has never shown any interest in lighting fires or torturing kittens.)

There's something about being on a journey, whether it's an uncomfortable bus ride or flying for hours in a seat squeezed between a fat man and opportunistic shoulder-sleeper, that I find calming. I think it has something to do with being able to let go, if just for a while, my need to control. I know my destination, I'm not responsible for getting me there, and I feel calm.

Pregnancy felt the same. One way or another, there would be a baby at the end and, even though I didn't have any guarantees about who that baby would be or even if he or she would be okay, once I was pregnant that background anxiety faded away.

Of course, I still suffered the usual paranoid worries of the newly pregnant. We bought a doppler on eBay and when I hadn't felt the baby's tumbles for a few hours I would run the scope across my belly until I heard the quick pattering of its heart.

The baby never kicked, just rolled and squirmed, and I would watch my stomach undulate and shift as I slothed on the couch at night.

Determined that I would have a drug-free, all-natural water birth – in the annoying manner of women who have never given birth before – I signed up with a local midwifery practice that offered me the same midwife the whole way through my pregnancy.

My midwife's last name was Minge. Really. And, while lovely, she seemed to have an automatic idea of who I was that turned out to be almost nothing like the reality.

I asked her to make sure there was a way to access drugs if things went badly and I decided I couldn't handle the pain.

'Oh, that won't happen. I can tell you want a relaxed, natural birth, and you will have one!' she said gaily.

'Right, but if things go badly – you know, just in case – would it take very long for the doctors to get down the hall with the drugs?'

Minge looked at me with disappointed eyes.

'Well, there is a point where it is all too late for that and you just have to push through until the baby is here,' she said.

I made her swear to let me know at least half an hour before we were near that spot.

•

It is here that perhaps we should stop for a second, before things get really real, so I can share just a few words of wisdom regarding the following:

Things that might give you anxiety during pregnancy and childbirth – a beginner's guide:

- It might take longer than one day to fall pregnant, in which case you will freak out that your eggs don't work or that you were born without a uterus. This fear will not lessen even after an ultrasound proves you have a uterus. Could be a phantom uterus.

- For the first twelve weeks of pregnancy you will worry about the baby falling out *a lot.* You will Google 'miscarriage' and lie awake at 3 a.m. thinking about all the miscarriages that happen all the time and whether all that cured meat you ate before you got pregnant could be doing bad things internally.

- A student midwife who hasn't had much experience with patients will become increasingly distressed while giving you a second-trimester scan before yelling, 'The baby has no spine!' (Unless this has been mentioned at one of the previous scans you have insisted on to make sure your baby has not been reabsorbed, you can safely ignore this one.)

- If you are unlucky enough to be struck down with one of the pregnancy complications – gestational diabetes, pre-eclampsia, hyperemesis – you will obsess and check your blood sugar/blood pressure/bottom-of-toilet-bowl umpteen times a day and panic about giving birth to a nineteen-pound baby that will get you on the news, or one of those tiny ones the size of a cigarette packet that people will then blame you for and they will secretly believe that you were also smoking things that come in tiny baby-size packets.

- After you give birth things may come out of you that look like organs. Apparently these are not organs, even though they are the size and shape and colour of a lung. Midwives and nurses will scoff and say, 'Better out than in' when you show them your faux-lung in the toilet.

- You will ask your husband to describe what he saw down there and he will clench his lips together until they go white and shake his head very quickly while tears slide down his face. This will not fill you with confidence.

- When you finally get pregnant again the doctor tells you your baby is breech and you will need a C-section. You feign disappointment but are secretly pleased you won't have to go through a natural birth again because you have heard they suck all the blood out during the surgery and that sounds really good.

— After your C-section you will feel totally fine with the idea of having to wear a catheter forever if it means you never have to stand up and feel your guts tip ominously forward against your stitches, threatening to blow out all over the person who brings your hospital-food dinner.

•

I didn't go into labour naturally (Mum reckons I was born almost three weeks late and when I finally came out I was old and wizened like 1990s Ronnie Corbett) and Minge offered me an induction to avoid a front-page-of-the-newspaper-sized baby.

'Yes!' I yelled before she had even finished the sentence. I was so sick of being pregnant and wanted this baby out where I could hold it. I had pictured the birth so often – the small drop of sweat on my brow that would slide down my cheek as I gave the few pushes, prettily, that would deliver my clean-skinned baby into the hands of his father. Josh would look at me, I would look at him, and a single tear of happiness would trickle shinily down my cheek. I would love my baby immediately and fiercely.

Minge looked mildly disappointed at my enthusiasm for the induction, as she still had me pegged as the all-natural, no drugs, down-on-all-fours, wait-till-the-baby-is-ready kind of new mother. I didn't want to disappoint her, and sort of fancied myself as a 'birth warrior', so I said I would still like to deliver in the birthing suite with the lights low and incense and soothing music, but could I perhaps also have the thing stuck in my hand for the drugs just in case I changed my mind?

I changed my mind.

It was all going along pretty smoothly, the pain not too bad, having a joke about bodily fluids in between contractions, until I got in the birthing pool. Until then I had wondered what all the fuss was about, had moaned a bit during contractions but also bunged it on a bit so Josh would think I was very strong to be bearing up so well despite enduring such terrible pain.

Maybe I really was one of those women who could give birth in a forest with just a deer looking on.

Then things escalated quickly, the pain increased by a factor of a million and I was screaming at them to get-me-out-of-the-bloody-bath and get-me-the-bloody-epidural-now.

The baby's head was stuck, grinding against my pelvis, and it was the worst pain I had ever felt. I didn't know how anyone survived this, so this pain could not be normal, must have meant dangerous things were happening inside me. Even when the epidural kicked in and the pain stopped I felt like I'd had the worst shock of my life. I didn't know it was possible to feel so bad and everything else I had ever felt, all those other times I was dying, paled in comparison.

Minge became stony-faced, running in and out of the room often; the final time she came back she was trailing behind a group of doctors who pulled out scalpels and forceps because my baby was distressed and I couldn't do this, couldn't get my baby out by myself.

When he was finally pulled from my body and placed on my chest – that moment I had imagined in the kind of detail and absurdity reserved for a Hollywood movie birth – I was already drawing away.

I knew everyone was watching me, or at least it felt like they were, so I made myself look at him, take in his red face and the chubby legs I hadn't expected. I kissed his head because it was what I was meant to do.

'Well, that's a head all right, no wonder he got stuck,' Minge said, tape in hand, and everyone laughed and I did too, in a series of huffs.

The surgeon swept out again, with a swarm of interns in his wake, and a young doctor stayed behind to sew me up. While she worked, Josh held our new baby, Sam, and the smile on his face was everything I wished I could feel. But I couldn't because that damned anxiety was back, licking its tongue at the bottom of my spine, whispering in my ear that I was trapped now, that I was dying.

I let the nurse hold my arm as I shuffled to the shower, where I sat on a plastic chair and she sprayed the muck away. I was so tired, but, more than that, so ruined – I felt like I had stared into the abyss and the level of ridiculous dramatic bullshit my anxiety was capable of was invisible to me. All I could hear was *deathdeathdeath*.

Mum and Dad came to meet Sam later that night. They called a quiet hello and then peered their heads around the corner of the curtain. Their faces showed all the things I wished I felt – love, rapture, wonder, joy – and they took it in turns to cuddle him, Sam tucked into the crooks of their arms while they looked up with happy eyes at me.

Mum wanted a pic of me holding him but I said my tummy was too sore, so I sat next to Josh while he cuddled Sam tight, a close-mouthed smile on my face because I knew good mothers loved their babies immediately and all I could feel was scared.

The thought that Mum might die and then what would become of me tortured me for years. It only really stopped when I had something to worry about more — my children.

23

New parenthood

As a young adult, ludicrously paranoid about being away from Mum lest something dreadful should befall her (and displaying all the signs of a ridiculously tenacious separation anxiety), I would call or text constantly to make sure she was okay. Arriving at Andy's house I would hunker down on the doorstep so that he wouldn't know that his 22-year-old girlfriend was calling the mother she had seen twenty minutes before to make sure she hadn't had a stroke or something.

'Hello, darling.'

'Oh, hi, yes, it's me and I was just ringing to make sure you are okay.'

'Yes, everything is fine.'

'So everything is fine then – nothing different? You feel all right?'

'Yes, everything is fine.'

'Okay. But you would tell me if you weren't, right? You wouldn't hide it because you thought it would make me feel better but really you are dying from cancer or something?'

'Why would I do that? Everything is fine.'

'Okay. Love you and you are the best mum ever. Don't forget that in case you die before I speak to you again.'

'I love you too. Bye.'

'Hang on a sec! Oh, okay, bye.'

A lot of this came from the belief that if something happened to Mum I would be so devastated, so torn, that I wouldn't be able to continue and would have to kill myself.

For someone who is terrified of death, I think you would call this being stuck between a rock and a hard place.

The thought that Mum might die and *then what would become of me* tortured me for years. It only really stopped when I had something to worry about more – my children.

After Sam was born I had a terrible time trying to bond with him. Traumatised by his birth and convinced that something terrible was happening with my body, which kept bleeding and aching and doing strange things that surely nobody as fragile as me could survive, I could not let myself love him. Couldn't love another thing that could die and hurt me. Didn't have room in my head for more worry and fear.

I searched the internet for all the terrible things that might be happening to me, and when my baby cried I shrivelled inside, couldn't bear the thought of holding him, of loving him.

I missed the early days of keen newborn eye-gazing and snuggling. Visitors piled up at the door and I didn't want any of them inside.

When the family next door finally wheedled their way in to marvel over the baby, like normal people do, the kind-faced wife asked me, 'Don't you just stare at him all day? Don't you love to watch him sleep?'

What could I say? A new mother is meant to be filled by her baby, fulfilled by her baby; her heart is meant to be full of love, complete. What kind of mother wishes she had never had her baby, wants her old life back so desperately that she shuts her ears to the cries of her child?

'I do, I love to watch him,' I whispered the lie back, but no one heard; instead, hands were in the cot, cooing and stroking and wondering.

Two friends laughed and knocked on the door for what seemed like hours, yelling through the letterbox slit, 'Let us in! We want to sniff your baby!' And I huddled around the corner until Sam let out a cry and I had to open the door.

I tried to smile and joke but felt like I was watching from another room as they held Sam and marvelled and cooed and wiped off his milky spew. I felt like everyone must see how badly I was struggling, and maybe it was there in their soft eyes, but I didn't feel it. I just felt so alone.

Another friend came with her husband and six-month-old to meet Sam, two weeks after he was born. We had been friends since school but things were often annoyingly competitive between us – we would find the smallest things to quibble over.

Again I forced the smiles and felt wretched as she tickled her daughter. When her husband went outside with Josh she asked me how I really was and I couldn't stop the pathetic tears, that I felt terrible and was a terrible, terrible mother.

I waited for her to tell me that it was normal, that she had felt the same, that everything would be okay.

'You know, my mum had a friend who felt like you when her daughter was born,' she said. 'She hated being a mother then and she hates it now. Some people just never love their children.'

Josh loved Sam for both of us in those early weeks. He cuddled and soothed and whispered and bathed and changed our baby. I sat, paralysed by anxiety and something else: the knowledge that there was no escape this time, no mapped route to the nearest exit, no avoidance strategy that could help me.

I would never have gone through with it, truly, but I made a deal with Josh about what would happen if it really did all get too much. He promised to take care of Sam if I left. Just having him say the words, to swear it, made me feel a little better, a little more in control.

Postnatal anxiety and depression are a bone-crushing combination of guilt and despair. I became so psychotically terrified of how destroyed I would be if anything happened to this baby I barely knew that I felt I couldn't afford to love him.

When Josh was out and I had to pick Sam up, I would envisage my arms going weak, his small body toppling from them onto the hard floor or, worse, onto a knife.

Sam smiled early, at just two weeks old, and I shudder to think it was some kind of survival instinct, some way to try to get me to connect with him, that he felt somehow that I wasn't really there.

Minge checked in often, sat on the couch and asked me if I was okay, and I nodded and said the right things about Sam's sleeping and feeding. But I would then tremulously ask her if she thought I might be dying. She listened to my fears, variations of the same ones every time, and told me I was okay, that everything was healing as it should, that there was plenty of support for me if I felt like I couldn't cope. But I didn't hear her. My body, always a source of unmitigated worry, was all over the shop, unpredictable, my recovery painful and messy.

And all the while, I knew my body was recovering from childbirth but I took its every vacillation as proof it was failing, that I couldn't afford to love my boy. That life was too fragile and loving him was too dangerous.

Mum and Josh dragged me to the doctor.

I told the doctor, matter-of-factly, why I couldn't bond with Sam, why it was too dangerous, why I felt I had made a terrible mistake.

He didn't pat me on the head, didn't tell me everything would be okay, didn't offer any assurances that we would make it through it all – whatever 'it all' is – alive.

'Elisa, if your baby dies it will be the worst thing that will ever happen to you,' he said. 'Your life as you know it will be over. There is no avoiding how destroyed your life would be if that happened.

'But how much worse would it be if you added the guilt of not being there for him, of not loving him, to that pain?'

This got through to my poor brain when all the other platitudes and reassurances that my baby would be fine had failed. That doctor's words stopped me from taking up my husband on the dreadful pact I had forced him to make.

Anxiety is simple minded. It is reptilian, base, primal. So it can be beaten with simplicity. When I worry about my boys now, when I see their tiny bodies and wonder at their fragility, I recite this mantra: *100 per cent of adults survived childhood.*

I know this is reductive. Obviously 100 per cent of adults surviving childhood automatically negates all the children who didn't. But reciting it to myself reminds me to look around, to see the hundreds, thousands, millions of people wandering around every day. People with sensitivities, disabilities, people who have suffered abuses and accidents, and they all made it.

I try to remind myself, using my rational brain and looking at evidence, that today making it through childhood – thanks to things like vaccines and other scientific advances, thanks to good food and education, and because I am lucky enough to live in a developed country – is normal.

All those people made it. There are no guarantees, but the odds are in our favour.

While anxiety sets you on edge, drives its nails into your shoulders and scrapes its teeth on your ribs, postnatal depression draws a grey cloak over your face, convinces you that nothing is worth the effort, and they can go hand in hand — postnatal anxiety and depression — a dreadful, ghoulish pair.

24

Postnatal anxiety and depression

Having a baby is intense. Really intense. Chuck in a traumatic birth or troubles breastfeeding or a baby who screams more than it sleeps or just the shock of there being a person where there wasn't one just the day before, and you are in prime mental illness territory.

The baby blues – when you get teary and cry for no apparent reason, feel a bit morose and exposed and overwhelmed – is common, super common: fifty to eighty-five per cent of women will experience this for a little time, maybe a week or two.

Postnatal depression is more; worse.

Support group Perinatal Anxiety & Depression Australia (PANDA) states that more than one in seven mothers will experience postnatal depression (PND) and, just so they don't feel left out, one in ten men will too.[1]

It's the rare (and lucky) new parent who doesn't feel some kind of worry or depression – having a baby is full-on! There's the sleep deprivation, the 'What the hell is in this nappy!?' moments, wondering if the screaming is normal, feigning sleep while the baby cries in the desperate hope your partner will fall for it so you don't have to bloody get up again.

However, if you freak out too much, all of those little things (and not so little things – babies poo all day) can become overwhelming and you might not find any moments in the day where you enjoy your baby, and you will feel guilty or desperately sad, or just so, so numb. And none of that is good.

If you're feeling overwhelmed or irritable or ashamed, or like you wish you could crawl out of your skin; if you're avoiding your baby, are restless and pace and pace and pace; if you can't sleep, even when the baby finally cries itself out and all is quiet; if you check the baby countless times a day to make sure it is okay, even if you only checked it minutes before and all was safe and well – all of these could be signs that something more than the 'baby blues' is at play. And if you feel that way for longer than two weeks, you might want to think about getting some extra help.

While anxiety sets you on edge, drives its nails into your shoulders and scrapes its teeth on your ribs, postnatal depression draws a grey cloak over your face, convinces you that nothing is worth the effort, and they can go hand in hand – postnatal anxiety and depression – a dreadful, ghoulish pair.

Postnatal depression may make you feel so ashamed that you can't lift your eyes from the ground, like you don't deserve your baby or partner, like there is no hope things will get better. You may be teary and confused and so very tired. You might draw away from friends, family, stop looking after yourself, stop eating, stop everything. You might want to run away from it all, escape your baby and your new life; you might worry eternally about something happening to your baby; you may wish you were dead and think of the ways you could make that happen.

Moreover, if a new mum is suffering, her partner's risk increases too.

It's hard, even without the added epic shittiness of anxiety or PND – new babyland is hard. But, thankfully, postnatal anxiety and PND are treatable.

Just some extra support around the house and with the baby might be enough; maybe counselling, maybe medication.

Some think PND is caused by the rapid change in hormones after birth, others believe that complications during pregnancy or delivery could be a factor, or that it is triggered by a family history of mood disorders. Research has found that having anxiety before pregnancy means you are more likely to develop PND but that treatment earlier in life may be preventative.[2]

Another study found that up to sixteen per cent of women experience a major depressive episode after birth and that these are more common in women with existing anxiety disorders.

The researchers found an improvement after treatment but didn't find any benefit in combining CBT with antidepressants, with paroxetine (an anti-depressant and anti-anxiety medication) alone proving equally efficacious.[3]

I needed medication. I didn't want it – I felt like an epic failure and worried it would hurt my baby through my milk. But a couple of weeks on it and the sun started to come out and I held Sam and saw him: really saw him, the dimple in his right cheek, the soft points of hair on his head, the way it was already thinning where it rubbed against his mattress.

I noticed his long fingers and how he hated the bath, but hated it a bit less if I was the one washing him. And I started to understand why people loved being parents, even if I couldn't live up to the ridiculously unreal expectations I had set for myself. I'm just not the gaze-at-the-sleeping-baby type of person, and that's okay too. It just took me a while to realise it didn't mean I loved him any less and the anxiety that had attached itself to the guilt like a limpet finally let go.

25

Parenting the anxious child

He gets more and more scared as the sun starts to go down.

As night falls, as dinner is picked at, he becomes quieter and quieter, until the questions start.

'Will I die?' he asks.

Not wanting to lie but knowing he is too young to understand the uncertainties of the world (I'm still not ready to accept them, either) I say, yes, we all die eventually but he won't die until he is an old, old man, even older than Grandma.

He considers this for a moment.

'Will my eyes shut forever when I die? Will you be with me?' And then his beautiful face folds and tears streak silently down his round cheeks, and despite all the years I have wondered and questioned and feared the same things,

I don't know how to help him and I wonder what on earth my anxiety was for, the years of introspection and idiocy, if I don't know how to help my boy.

So I reassure, I cuddle. When frustrated, I tell him to stop being silly, but, just like my mum could never convince me I was safe – from the drowning hole, from disease, from embarrassment – I can't get him to believe that everything is all right.

Always sensitive, Sam's anxieties seem, horribly, to closely mirror my own. My fear of the drowning hole is mirrored by his fear of floods, that he will be engulfed or washed away.

•

When Sam started school last year we chose a Catholic school, not because we are religious but because they put on a good private school for a fraction of the cost of the posh ones.

Sam's school is tiny and sweet but, for the first time, he has heard about traditions like Easter and crucifixion and nails and bleeding and rising again, and it is all particularly terrifying for the anxious five-year-old brain with a tendency towards literalism and melodrama.

In the second week of school his teacher pulled me aside to tell me that Sam had scratched another little boy.

He was spending every recess and lunch in the doorway of the boys' toilet because, in his first week, he had seen a group of kids mucking around, seeing who could get the soapiest hands and make suds spill out of the drain in the middle of the floor. To Sam, these 'bubble floods' were enormous tsunamis capable of washing him away. Through shaking tears he told me he had to watch to make sure that the bubbles didn't keep rising, didn't spill out of the bathroom and into the playground where they would inundate his classroom and kill him.

One week he was convinced that the bubbles were capable of becoming so powerful that they would take over the world and wash all of the country's scorpions to him, then they would sting him to death. About to scoff – and how heartless of me to even think of dismissing his fears when I have been controlled by a litany of the ludicrous – I had to show him why that was impossible. At the end he nodded sadly, though I could tell it was more in an effort to mollify me than because of any real relief he felt.

Sam lives much of his life in his mind. After school and on weekends he will spend hour after hour bent over pages of blank paper, filling them with elaborate maps and game designs. When he is happy with his plans he will rope his dad into a game of magic or some other rough boy-game, but if it deviates from his idea of what should happen he will dissolve into tears or tantrum. He wants to control his world as much as I do mine.

Sam was a very 'good' baby – 'one out of the box' was how my dad described him. He didn't cry as much as I heard the other mums say was usual for their kids, was easily soothed with a cuddle and a whispered word, smiled early and often.

Yet he was sensitive too. Scared to try new things. He still is.

A new food on his plate will send him into a rictus of disgust; if forced to try something he will often vomit it straight back up, screaming it is too soft or rough or pointy or *yuckyyuckyyucky*.

At kinder-gym, as other kids raced around and climbed to the top of the bars to the proud-terror of their parents, Sam would climb one or two rungs before wailing for me to rescue him. If a bigger child muscled him out the way when he was playing with a new toy, he would actually shake with rage, his fists clenched and juddering at his sides.

When Sam was three we started taking him to Little Athletics because he is clumsy and skinny and we thought he would like it.

It was hot and bright on the oval, and as the other kids charged about, yelling and boisterous, Sam hid behind my legs, refusing to even try a race or throw a ball. He cried and cried, increasingly hysterical and obstinate, and I felt like the worst kind of mean mum but also so frustrated that I just wanted to grab him and shout in his tiny face – so like my own – 'WHY CAN'T YOU JUST BE NORMAL? DO YOU KNOW HOW ANXIOUS YOU MAKE ME? JUST BE LIKE THE OTHERS!'

I don't want Sam to spend as much of his life worried as I have. I want him to embrace life, bask in it; I want him to learn to roll with the punches, to accept the occasional sadness and mayhem that comes with a life well lived.

However, the techniques I use are too much for a small boy, I can't expect him to sit with his anxiety while a flood comes thundering towards him. Can't expect him to understand why such a flood is unlikely or how I will always do my very best to keep him *safesafesafe*.

Instead, my husband and I, we try to think like him.

When Sam is starting to panic, we ask him to look for evidence and solutions. He is interested in science, has talked for years about wanting to be a 'submarine builder' when he grows up, so we talk about being scientists, about looking for the reasons behind how things work. We challenge his fear with reality.

When his fear of bubble floods rears its head we talk about how weak bubbles are; we make some out of detergent and get him to smash them and talk about how easy it is; we point out drains in the street and show him where water goes after it rains.

We encourage him to be observant about happy things too – to get down close to the ground to notice the way the earth cracks in the summer, to describe a weird bug on a bushwalk, to answer his own questions about the world by paying attention to what really *is*.

His fear of death is trickier and, ironically, we have chosen to rely on a Catholic tradition to sooth our not-very-religious child (although I often hear him whisper, 'Dear God, please bring me more Pokémon', from the back seat when I drive him home from school). We tell him that when he dies, when he is an old, old man, even older than Grandma, he will go to Heaven and we will all be there waiting for him. The enormity of death and oblivion is too scary for me, let alone a five-year-old.

When the anxiety still curls in his tummy, scratching at his throat with needled claws, we talk about Dudley Danger. He knows being anxious sometimes is good. That it keeps him safe and well. We all have it. But when his anxiety is going crazy we tell him Dudley Danger is being silly.

It's something I read – that giving his anxiety a name so he can see its face and push it away helps to deny it power, to take that power back as his own.

Sometimes this works, sometimes it doesn't. If we can make Dudley look especially silly and stupid, if we can make Sam laugh by pretending to push Dudley into a puddle or sweep him into the bin, all the better.

Sometimes the best we can do is distract him with a movie, get him running and laughing, start to plan his birthday party even though it is months off – anything to chase the shadows away.

He still climbs into bed with us on some nights, some weeks more than others, and I often don't even know he is there until morning, he cuddles in so quietly and lies absolutely still.

Then he will whisper, 'It's morning' in the grey light and I will turn around and kiss his cheek.

And we ask each other, in hushed voices, what wonderful things might happen today.

Getting little ones to be more like detectives or scientists with their thoughts is a new way of approaching childhood anxiety.

26

How to help the anxious child

Realising, eventually, that telling Sam over and over that his fears were not real and wouldn't happen was achieving precisely nothing – in much the same way that constant reassurances mollify my own anxieties for an hour or two at best before my brain finds a way around the soothing words and the anxieties rush back in – I thought about how to harness his imagination and curiosity in ways that might help.

It has turned out that what we encourage him to do – be a scientist – is not very different from what experts today suggest kids do when suffering anxiety.

Getting little ones to be more like detectives or scientists with their thoughts is a new way of approaching childhood anxiety. Asking them to collect evidence and look for facts, rather than get lost and overwhelmed in the scary what-ifs, is an advisable approach.

And with this, even with kids, we see again the importance of facing, not fleeing from, fear.

Gently, gradually, when kids face what frightens them, their anxiety improves significantly.

In a time when parents are becoming more restrictive, controlling, when no one wants to admit to being a helicopter parent despite many of us being a bit – or a lot – that way inclined, the advice is to let kids get messy, play in the dirt, and learn that it is good to face tricky, dirty, yucky situations.

Child anxiety has been the focus of much examination and research. A recent US study found that picky eating in small children, even at moderate levels, was associated with increased risk of depression and anxiety in later years.[1] Moderate cases have also been associated with symptoms of separation anxiety and ADHD.

Could this be a variation of disgust sensitivity?

When he was younger, Sam could become so worked up about eating something he found yucky that he would vomit. Is this a sign that he has inherited my disgust sensitivity? Or does he really just not like corn?

A significant association has also been found between maternal anxiety disorder status and negative expectations of child coping, behaviour which can affect the way affected mothers, in turn, parent. Treatments for childhood anxiety disorders, when found alongside parental anxiety disorder, may benefit from specific targeting of parents' anxious thinking styles.[2]

After ADHD, anxiety is the most common type of psychological distress reported by kids and teens, with around 7 per cent of children and adolescents diagnosed in a 12-month period.[3]

University of Queensland child anxiety researcher and clinical psychologist Dr Vanessa Cobham said in an interview that I conducted with her that, while it can be a problem earlier, anxiety is usually identified as a problem around the age of six.

'There is an innate temperamental quality called behavioural inhibition that has been found to put infants at increased risk of developing an anxiety disorder as children,' she says.[4]

CBT is the treatment of choice when it comes to many anxious children, but some studies have found that its effectiveness can be tied to certain factors. It might be less successful for girls, and it is tied to the severity of the primary anxiety if another mood disorder is suffered at the same time. But age and parental mental illness are not significant.[5]

For Sam, however – unlike the kids of my generation and before – there is now real hope for effective intervention.

'Research in this field really began to take off in the late 1980s,' says Dr Cobham.

'Probably the biggest change is that researchers and clinicians have become increasingly aware that the vast majority of anxious children who could benefit from intervention are never receiving any type of intervention. So, this is probably our biggest challenge – how to increase our capacity to reach the kids who need help.

'Parents are the most important people in their children's lives and there are lots of things that they can do to help. Parents can help their anxious kids to face up to their fears in a graduated way. They can help their children to learn how to solve problems for themselves – thinking through all the possible alternatives in terms of how they might respond to a problem, the likely consequences of each alternative.'

Also, ask the professionals for help.

I spoke to a child psychologist, my cousin Simon, when Sam started freaking out at Little Athletics and I didn't know whether it was kinder to make him keep going or to let him quit – of course, the answer was to persist. Avoidance is never the key, not even for kids.

In the grand tradition of my family, Simon also has anxiety but is the last person you would ever suspect of suffering it.

He is funny and tall, with a round, smiling face and a laugh you can hear when you leave the table for the loo; for most of my early childhood I was convinced I would marry him.

Having lived a childhood relatively free of anxiety – only remembering throwing up with nervousness a few times before going into bat at cricket – Simon had his first massive panic attack at thirty-three.

'Soaking sweat, nausea, diarrhoea and many other glamorous symptoms,' he says in an email to me.[6]

'Followed by six months more of panic attacks. Bad enough that I had six months off work.'

One year seeing another psychologist, two years on anti-anxiety medication, and lifestyle changes like working less, sorted him out.

'Upon reflection, the causes were an accumulation of several major stressors over three years and an inherited vulnerability – death of a mentor and dear friend, taking over the work and patients of my mentor while grieving at the same time, my eighteen-month-old daughter involved in a medical emergency in country South Australia that meant she had to be helicoptered back to Adelaide, then further hospital admissions via ambulance over the next few years, me working too many hours and never saying no to a referral even when I was fully booked already.'

Now forty-seven, he hasn't had a single panic attack for twelve years and knows to keep an eye out for a single symptom – the twinge in the chest muscle – that tells him he has been working too much or is getting too tired or stressed.

I asked him what I should do for Sam when my son refused to run with the other kids at athletics – asked whether I should stop and try again in a year – and Simon told me that the very worst thing would be to let Sam quit.

I shouldn't force him to participate but he had to be there. Had to sit with me and watch the other kids having fun, watch them jumping into the long jump pit, see how far they could throw beanbags; be there as they bounced on the high jump mat and thirstily gulped water and shrieked when they got a sticker at the end.

Within a month Sam was racing the others, trailing behind in the 200 metres with the kids who got distracted by a butterfly or stopped to look at a dog being walked past; being bossy and stopping other kids pushing in when it wasn't their turn at beanbag shotput, standing gleefully in line for his sticker.

•

A 2012 Australian study looked for common indicators in young children to see if middle-childhood anxiety could be predicted. By looking at a group of four-year-olds and then reassessing them when they were nine, researchers found that behavioural inhibition, maternal anxiety, and maternal overinvolvement were significant predictors of clinical anxiety.[7]

Given the importance of maternal anxiety as a predictor, they recommended decreasing the mother's anxiety through exposure and cognitive restructuring. Their findings highlighted the important role mothers play in affecting child anxiety through their own anxiety and their parenting, their over-protectiveness.

I have two boys. The oldest is me all over again, much to my dismay. He has the same fears without me ever voicing mine to him.

The youngest – who benefitted from a second-time mum, but the same mum nonetheless – is a different beast. Confident, brash, cheeky, physical, strong, Edward is calm like his dad, seemingly impervious to the danger Sam sees everywhere.

When Sam gets nervous and I start to remind him about looking for the facts, Edward will pipe up in his tiny voice, 'Be a scientist', and Sam will get cross and tell him, 'Shhh'.

I hope Edward is like his dad, I hope he never feels the anxiety Sam feels. And I hope, more than anything, that Sam can learn to think through his anxiety, bear it, and come out the other side, without losing all of the beautiful things that have come with his sensitivity: his detailed drawings, the way he can lose himself in his pencils for hours, the way he tries so very hard, all the time; his imagination, though wild, and his exuberance, the way he can go from sleeping to leaping in a moment. His beautiful, sensitive, Sam heart.

Other Stories

N is small and beautiful and kind and I was always jealous of her because her life is fabulous and she makes it all look easy.

She has anxiety.

Anxiety is one of those terms I never really applied to myself but it's something I've always grappled with. As a child I'd lie awake at night worrying about death – most often my parents', sometimes my own. And I'd cry. And I'd panic. I always thought I was just weird. In fact, it's only been recently, with anxiety as a condition becoming more freely discussed, that I've matched the word with the feeling. And I've been relieved to discover that perhaps I'm not a complete nut, there are others like me.

My tendency to overthink, constantly worry and continuously play out scenarios as a child developed over the years into a continuous buzzing in my ear, a constant poke in the ribs.

It's an ongoing conversation I have with myself about my next move, my last move, a moment five years ago, or a moment five years in the future. An over-analysis of every aspect of my life, an ability to turn happiness into fear, joy into sadness and become perpetually confused about what is the 'right' thing to do.

The main trigger for my anxiety is silence (where my mind takes over), such as when I'm driving, lying in bed or sitting at my computer. The other trigger, bizarrely, is moments of joy. Enjoying a special moment with my mum will almost always bring about a minor panic attack at the thought of having these moments taken from me. How many do I have left? How will I cope without them?

Special moments with my children leave me fearing the hand of time – my kids are getting older, how many cuddles do I have left, what will our adult relationship be like? It's the constant questioning – is my marriage the best it can be? Is my work/life balance okay? Am I making the most of my life, which is almost half over – you get the picture!

I don't have great coping mechanisms. Distraction sometimes helps, as does verbalising my insanely repetitive thoughts to my mum, who says the right thing each and every time. Mums are the best. Those who are happy to listen to the rambling deserve a medal.

While still prone to overreacting and imaginitis and catastrophising, the scatteredness I have always felt, the constant feeling of agitation and nervousness for no reason, has subsided. I feel more 'in' myself.

27

The future

When you've been anxious for a long time, when you've tried a bazillion different treatments but haven't found that magic salve – the forever cure-all – you get to the point where you'll try just about anything.

Which is why, in the name of research but also because I have not given up hope of quashing this anxiety forever and for good (and somehow changing what, by this stage, just seems a fixture of my flawed personality), I tried to get a faecal transplant.

This, in very base terms, would mean putting someone else's poo up my bum.

Of course, it is slightly more complicated than that. Before a transplant can be performed, the 'donor' has to be tested for pathogens and other things that would make you sicker than when you started, and then the poo is churned or something equally unreadable-for-the-squeamish before being inserted into the lower intestine via the rectum (or sometimes to the gut via a nasal-gastric tube, but even I have my limits).

Faecal Microbiota Transplant (FMT) is already being used very effectively for a notoriously difficult-to-treat recurrent infection – clostridium difficile (c. diff.) – which causes very serious diarrhoea and can be fatal.

Still experimental, the treatment has approval for use in the United States of America for patients with serious c. diff. infection who are able to give informed consent.

One institution – Emory University – has performed more than 120 faecal microbiota transplants under very strict conditions for recurrent c. diff. infections, with a more than 90 per cent success rate.

Recently the therapy has been suggested as a way to possibly treat mental health disorders. By now you've probably heard lots about the mind–gut connection. That the gut has over 100 million neurons and many contain the same neurotransmitters as the brain. That the diversity of the bacteria in the gut might influence everything from your tendency to be fat despite eating the same food as the skinny person next to you[1], to the development of allergies.[2]

The theory behind FMT for the treatment of anxiety or depression or other mental illnesses is, basically, that introducing 'non-anxious' bacteria to the gut of the anxious could alter their microbiome – introducing more of the types of bacteria associated with a lack of anxiety – and cure their mental illness.

Sounds great to me! I even had a willing donor: my husband. The calmest man alive, Josh has already seen me give birth and we have eaten street food while travelling through developing countries together and suffered the attendant fallout, so if we were going to repulse each other it would have happened a long time ago.

Wondering if this could be my magical cure, I started calling around. And, like so many things that seem too good (and easy) to be true, the news, at least for now, was not good.

Sadly, like so many 'miracle' treatments you hear about, FMT is still a long way from being a recognised or endorsed treatment for anxiety.

Professor Jane Andrews, a gastroenterologist at the Royal Adelaide Hospital, says that while there are lots of theories floating around about the link between the gut and mental health, there is, so far, little human data.

'We do know that there is a very active two-way communication between the gut and the brain, as evidenced by the fact that anxiety can make people perceive gut symptoms and make existing symptoms worse, and that psychological therapy (like CBT/hypnotherapy) is very effective to reduce gut symptoms (proven in IBS and functional dyspepsia),' she says in an email.[3]

'It is unknown, however, whether the gut microbiome is involved in this two-way communication of symptoms.

'For lesions (visible abnormalities in the gut) it is unclear if there is any link between the gut and mental health. We do know, however, that if you have a gut disease like inflammatory bowel disease you have a higher risk of a mental health issue – like anxiety, depression, stress – but this might be only because you have a chronic disease and might not be gut specific.'

As yet, no particular strain of gut bacteria has been identified as being protective against mental illness and Professor Andrews says there are no 'signs on the horizon yet' of one.

She advocates methods already tested and proven to be a part of the lives of people less likely to have a mental health disorder: eating a healthy diet, being a normal weight, not smoking, and exercising regularly. These are also all things that can influence the gut microbiome.

'So maybe the best advice we can give people thus far is simple advice to follow existing health guidelines,' says Professor Andrews. 'I know people want "magical" solutions but the old advice is still probably the best we have. The microbiome is not magic and it doesn't live in a vacuum – it lives in people – and if you eat rubbish, smoke, don't exercise and are overweight you won't have a healthy microbiome and taking a simple probiotic won't change that. You need to change the ecosystem and to do that you need to change the inputs.

'A good lifestyle, diet, avoiding antibiotics when they are not needed, and not smoking. There is no proof [that probiotics help], it's best to change the ecosystem by changing inputs.'

She doesn't, however, rule out FMT being used to treat mental illness in the future; the biggest barrier at the moment being dodgy practitioners doing FMT outside of studies and without publishing data as needed for proper evidence gathering – basically charging patients for an unproven therapy for commercial gain.

Dr Antonina Mikocka-Walus, a health psychology expert from the University of York, agrees that the idea behind FMT for mental illness is a novel one but shares concerns about the lack of evidence so far.

'Like Jane, I think physical activity, diet, not smoking, et cetera are the current recommendations to follow,' she says in another email, invited to join the conversation by Professor Andrews.[4]

'I would add social support, as in many psychological studies it comes as a factor equal to smoking (as a risk factor). To me it is truly fascinating that lack of social support may pose exactly the same risk to health as smoking.'

Julie Norem, author of *The Positive Power of Negative Thinking*, is moving forward with her investigations too. With a developing body of research into the benefits of negative mood, especially on specific kinds of cognitive processing – there's evidence that people in a mildly negative mood are less likely to stereotype and are less gullible – Norem's current study is looking at whether defensive pessimists overall are less likely to stereotype and less likely to succumb to a number of other cognitive biases.

Work is being done by others on the effect of oestrogen levels on women's emotional health. Low levels are thought to make some women more vulnerable to trauma at some points of their menstrual cycle as the hormone naturally fluctuates. Research suggests that high levels can be partially protective against emotional disturbance. Birth control pills might one day be able to be used to prevent post-traumatic stress.[5]

Connections between connective tissue disorders that affect the strength of joints and integrity of the spine and anxiety have been made. Joint hypermobility syndrome – which can range from mild to disabling – can lead to overstimulation of the sympathetic nervous system because the spinal column may be compressed in some people when the head tips up – this can be seen in affected individuals in the dentist's chair or with their head leaning back over the hairdresser's basin. Severe whiplash can cause anxiety symptoms that mimic those suffered by those with connective tissue disorders.

There is also a growing body of work in the fields of nutrigenomics and nutrigenetics looking into the effect of nutrition on mental health. Specifically, there has been an increasing amount of talk around MTHFR mutations and their possible role in mental illness.

MTHFR, or methylenetetrahydrofolate reductase, seems to be the hyped gene mutations of the last few years, implicated in everything from stroke to multiple miscarriages to certain cancers.

Its link to anxiety is not broadly supported by evidence-based studies at the moment – which makes me hesitant to share my own experience.

I am very far from anti-science. I give my children *all* the vaccines. I know homeopathy is bollocks. I believe in rigorous and replicable scientific studies.

Yet, for me, treating the possible deficiency caused by a variation in my MTHFR has lessened my anxiety.

Is this a placebo?

I don't think so, but can't rule it out. I have tried other treatments I actually believed might work that did nothing, when I thought taking vitamins wouldn't help at all but they did.

The theory behind the treatment seems promising. A blood test ordered by my GP showed that my MTHFR gene was a bit wonky (scientific term). I have variations in the MTHFR enzyme gene that mean I cannot convert folic acid to folinic acid very quickly at all; my doctor estimates the conversion happens around 70 per cent slower than most (90 per cent) of people.

Folinic acid is used to produce serotonin and also dopamine and noradrenalin to regulate mood and prevent anxiety, as well as removing homocysteine (a chemical that plays an important role in mood regulation). The gene problem predisposes me to depression, anxiety, and elevated homocysteine levels which, in turn, predispose me to heart and vascular disease.

A by-product of folinic acid generation is 5MTHF, which is used by the body to help with DNA division and vascular regulation. Slow production of this can cause migraines and miscarriage.

To bypass this problem, all I need to do is take folinic acid (the bioavailable form of folic acid – essentially skipping the dodgy gene) and methylcobalamin B12. That's it.

The link between MTHFR mutations, mood disorders and neurodevelopmental problems are not new to science. Studies have suggested that homocysteine levels might predict the length someone might suffer from post-traumatic stress disorder[6], and that an MTHFR mutation is associated with major depression, bipolar disorder and schizophrenia.[7]

A study in Northern Ireland found a MTHFR variation was associated with an increased risk of depressive episodes.[8]

A 2011 study reported a possible link between a different MTHFR variation and attention deficit hyperactivity disorder (ADHD).[9]

A study in Arkansas, published in *Molecular Psychiatry*, found that a group of children with autism who were treated with folinic acid showed significant improvements in verbal communication, receptive and expressive language, attention, and stereotypical behaviour. Approximately one-third of treated children demonstrated moderate to much improvement.[10]

However, there doesn't seem to be a whole lot of consensus on the importance of the existence of an MTHFR mutation in someone with anxiety. Trying to find a comprehensive study that looks at the possible link between MTHFR variations and anxiety is tricky, even though its link to other mood disorders is extensively researched.

My GP is convinced there is a link – he tested me for the mutation and has driven my treatment, which included regulating my circadian rhythms so my brain had a chance to regenerate serotonin levels. After years of terrible rest, I now sleep soundly. But plenty of other doctors think it is questionable and won't explore this avenue until more research has been done.

It is true that there haven't been any conclusive studies done so far that prove that the mutation's role in anxiety is important or otherwise. But my doctor was of the opinion that treating it would work and the worst that could happen, if I took the vitamins, was that my body wouldn't need the supplement and would wee it out.

I was sceptical. I'm not a fan of 'woo' and am a firm believer in the scientific method and the importance of research and replicable studies. But my bodily response to the vitamins was undeniable. My inner turmoil changed.

While still prone to overreacting and imaginitis and catastrophising, the scatteredness I have always felt, the constant feeling of agitation and nervousness for no reason, has subsided. I feel more 'in' myself. I acknowledge that this is not scientific evidence; this is pure anecdote.

It has not cured my anxiety. But it has lessened it markedly. I noticed it, the change. Those who love me have noticed it. When I become anxious now it ebbs as quickly as it arrives. No longer does the adrenaline circle endlessly around my body, tearing at my limbs, trying to find a place, a reason, to swell. The most noticeable change, for me, is my new ability to find calm again so soon after anxiety has torn through my chest. And the constant background burr, the hum of dis-ease, is gone.

It's all swings and roundabouts when you have anxiety. Life is going well, you're off the meds, feeling fab, when that tiny flicker of anxiety starts to whisper in your stomach. It might not even be anything major that sets it off. Maybe a crap day at work, maybe the kids are being extra annoying, maybe you catch a glimpse of yourself in the mirror and the light is bad and you look like Worzel Gummidge. Whatever it is, that trigger, the anxiety starts again.

For years I ignored mine when it started up again because I wanted to be cured. I want anxiety to have buggered off forever and when I feel its dirty smear I am disappointed and

I feel guilty that I am still mental, and I want so very, very badly for it not to be true.

When I went back to the doctor in the autumn of 2014 – the visit that led to being tested for MTHFR variations – my anxiety had slyly crept up on me and I hadn't realised it had become so bad, even though many mornings I couldn't get out of bed because I was stuck to the mattress with tears and terror.

Josh would be up with the boys, dressing them and feeding them, while I quivered beneath the doona. When he went to leave the house for work the tears would come and I felt so useless but also hoped desperately that he would see how useless I was and would stay home and do the things I couldn't do, which was everything.

That is not me any more.

Maybe folinic acid is a placebo – until more studies are done on MTHFR we won't know either way – but I don't want to go back there.

And the treatment doesn't stand alone for me. After all this time, after decades of search and trial and error and those pure, cool moments of calm found in between the sharp cuts of anxiety, I have found what works for me.

Combined with all the other things I have learned about my anxiety – where it may have sprung from, what sharpens its claws and increases its hold, where to turn when it seems insurmountable – I have also learned what makes it small.

What I need to do when it tries to knock me down again.

Other Stories

A is only young, nineteen, but was diagnosed with generalised anxiety disorder almost a decade ago. She is articulate and brave – so very brave.

I have (officially) suffered from generalised anxiety disorder (GAD) since I was ten years old. I had my first panic attack at nine years old. I thought I was dying. I am now nineteen and pretty sure I'm still 'dying'. At least now I know what from.

When I first suffered a panic attack I genuinely thought I must have been having a heart attack. I was too little to understand or recognise any of my symptoms, and the fact that it came out of the blue while we were watching a movie in class made no sense to me, so I couldn't think of any other explanation. I was scared to tell my mum I thought I might be dying, but I didn't have a choice. I described my heart beating too fast to be normal, and saying, 'I really feel like I'm going to die'. I was taken to my GP who has known me since birth. We looked for physical symptoms and had my heart checked. When we finally realised it was panic attacks I was suffering from I knew it wouldn't be easy to overcome and would take several years.

After recognition of my panic attacks, they only got worse. I now believe my generalised anxiety developed from a panic disorder. By the next year of school, now grade five and ten years old, I couldn't go on school camp without Dad and couldn't do sleepovers or birthday parties without panicking or being with a parent. The dependence I had on the safety net of my parents led to a severe separation anxiety that saw my absence for approximately fifty per cent of grade six.

No one knows what anxiety feels like when they haven't experienced it for themselves. You get sick of hearing 'don't worry', 'I get stressed sometimes too', and 'I'm so worried about the test tomorrow too'. In fact, you get *physically* sick of hearing it, because all these things make you anxious too. I have never felt so alone in my life.

It's an indescribably irrational feeling when you are certain beyond doubt that when someone leaves your sight they may as well be dead. It is just as irrational to completely believe this and let it control your life. My anxiety was at a point where I couldn't let my parents out of my sight. This included going to school, bedtime, family holidays, shopping, parties, any time, you name it. I was in agony in my mind every day waking up knowing what I had to face that day. There was no relief at bedtime thinking

I'd accomplished a whole day. No relief no matter what. I couldn't sleep, I couldn't breathe, I could barely leave the house. Sometimes I'm thankful I was only eleven.

I knew I was hurting my parents. They couldn't do anything without me, my mother couldn't go to work some days and was late nearly every day of the week. I witnessed her cry over the phone about me and be frustrated beyond belief. I felt so guilty that I had no control over it but I couldn't change my anxiousness. On several occasions where I 'lost' Mum and Dad, I became so fragile I couldn't leave their side for days, it was like going through trauma.

Medication was never a consideration due to its powerful nature and the fact I was only eleven when I started therapy. I was sure cognitive behavioural therapy would be the death of me because it failed every time and is not a long-term solution for me. I went from psychologists to psychiatrists and never felt I was getting better.

As I transitioned to high school, a nurturing, independent, all-girls school, I started to find my people. People who supported me and made me feel safe at school everyday. I finally found my footing and was happy for the first time in a long time.

However, after several years of feeling 'fine' it manifested again at about age sixteen. By now I was fearful of other things, I could do sleepovers and stay home alone, but parties and alcohol scared the hell out of me.

Since then I have been seeing one psychologist who has been an absolute miracle to my mentality. She works on long-term strategies and feels the same way I do about CBT. I have long-term goals to overcome my severe claustrophobia, specifically of lifts, as well as travel anxiety and a few other issues.

I don't think my anxiety will ever leave me, I don't think it leaves anyone completely.

I still have relapses occasionally into days of waking up with anxiety, living with anxiety all day, and not being able to sleep because of anxiety. It will always be part of who I am but now I have the strength and positivity to cope with it and be happy, as well as do things that 'normal' people do.

Although I said at the beginning that I still feel like I'm dying, I feel like I'm dying but I can delay the death if I put my mind to it, and that's all it takes.

The key is no more running away.

The key is exploration.

The key is acceptance.

The key is hope.

28

Today

I woke up the other morning, alone, and my phone said it was 7.46 a.m. but it was completely dark.

With two young sons who creep regularly into our bed in the small hours, most mornings are spent squashed to the side of the mattress, one arm clasped desperately to the edge to avoid falling out as one son starfishes in the middle, the other lies horizontally across the pillows, and my husband snores on, unmolested.

Someone will cry 'OW' before 6 a.m., at least half an hour will be spent telling everyone to 'SHHH', before they succeed in bullying their father into getting up to satisfy demands for toast, milk and ABC4Kids.

But this morning there is silence and it is now 7.48 a.m. and I am alone. The normally busy road outside is still, no birds sing, and the small burr of anxiety starts in the pit of my stomach and I know, am certain, that the sun has failed to come up today.

That this is the end of days.

Yes, yes, I know this is patently ridiculous – you'd imagine an alarm or at least some kind of general public hysteria if the sun had, in fact, burned itself out while we slept, but it took only moments for the anxiety to convince me that the fantastical had occurred, that this was the most likely reason it was still dark and not the far more prosaic and correct reason: that my phone was stuffed.

And straightaway, my old defence mechanisms jumped in. Instead of getting out of bed to see where everyone was, I lay there and stared at the ceiling, because the only thing worse than doing that would be to get up and find that everyone was dead or gone and life was ruined forever.

In my grown-up bed in my grown-up house I am two again, and the drowning hole is now a sun that won't rise and if I lie here long enough, if I think about it, pour all of my energy into it, I can find the way through, the escape hatch, salvation.

Of course, the sun did rise.

After a while the light in my room changed to grey, the birds started up, I heard the squeal of one of my boys as the other chased him down the hall to my room from the spare bed where all three of my loves had decamped, one by one, during the night. In they tumbled, squalling dreams about Jabba the Hutt involved in some terrible battle with Spiderman and multiple Ninja Turtles.

Cars drove by, a bus. And my phone bleeped error at me before changing itself to the correct time.

And my heart unclenched and my brain whispered, *Stupid but be alert next time too, just in case*, and I wondered if tomorrow would bring something better.

I haven't feared the drowning hole, the deep bottomless muck of it, for many years. But its essence, its true form, has stayed with me. In many ways, I think it has made me who I am.

At two, the drowning hole was the manifestation of what cowed me, then and now – the true root of my anxiety: that nothing is certain.

Not knowing for sure what comes next is, for me and so many others, terrifying. Maybe for you too. And seeking control is to fight the ultimate losing battle.

Instead of using this knowledge to live in the moment, to live every moment as if it is my last (as the annoying self-helpers suggest is so very easy to do), I have instead spent my life looking for the loopholes, the cracks, the things I can do to make sure I am safe, the ones I love are safe, that we won't have just *this* moment of being okay, but every moment.

I think, without a doubt, that much of my anxiety is genetic. Its intractability, its persistence in the face of so many treatments, its passage through my ancestors to my door bellow that this is so.

I doubt I will ever be able to say that I am anxiety free; that I am cured forever. But I have learned a thing or two.

I know, now, the things that help quieten my anxiety. And I know, in those moments when it escapes its bonds and takes over my body, tears at my lungs and heart with hot claws, that there are ways to trap it once more.

Much of this is to accept that there are no guarantees.

There is no way to ensure that the life you have – I have – will be safe and grief-free and painless.

What I have learned through the writing of this book and almost forty years, is that the lengths we go to try to fool ourselves into thinking we can stop bad things happening are an illusion, and a dangerous one at that.

I don't know what your answer is. God, I barely know mine.

But I know that, to begin, I had to face all of the things I have been running away from for so long. I needed to stop making deals with the universe – that if I make it to the door before it swings shut my children will be safe, that if I can make it home from the supermarket without being stopped by any red lights I will never get sick and die. Magical thinking helps no one, is the preserve of the child, traps your mind in a place where it believes that obsession and fear is the same as action and understanding.

Avoidance is the worst thing you can do when you are anxious. It is the thing that has made my anxiety more tenacious, more debilitating, more terrifying than anything else I have done.

Being aware of how I avoid things makes it easier to undo a lifetime's habit. Not easy, but easier. Along with just being so sick of myself that I am willing to try anything to lessen the load of anxiety without thinking it will change who I intrinsically am.

A major first step is acceptance. The years I have wasted looking at those around me who appear to coast through life without worrying over every breath, who can travel and love and work, and only feel anxious when the occasion deserves it, not all the time. Oh, what I wouldn't give to be one of them.

But I'm not. I'm just not. I am obsessive and literal and sensitive and highly strung, and I react to things others don't. Even if I can cure specific phobias, others will take their place. It has happened before and will happen again. But if I accept that this is me and try to still live the most enjoyable life I can, that is okay too, and probably a lot less pointless than railing against the realities of life as me.

There are other things too. Along with avoiding avoidance (Ha!) is exposure. If I feel a new fear emerging I can stop it in its tracks by planting my face in it. A body isn't capable of maintaining extreme stress eternally – it will calm down. The secret is staying with the fear, facing the source, until the anxiety wanes and your brain learns that there was nothing to fear there in the first place, like the childhood monster under the bed that dissolved when you worked up the courage to lift the edge of the doona and peer underneath.

And there are all the things that doctors seem to recommend to everyone, mostly because they work. I exercise, and being massively uncoordinated I like to dance or do something equally impossible so my brain is as involved as my body.

Distraction is a marvellous thing. A good book. A stupid movie. Anything that takes your mind out of your body, where it searches eternally for the source of your anxiety, and fixes it outwards.

I meditate. I've tried countless types and the ones where you are supposed to empty your mind are patently ridiculous. My doctor suggested transcendental meditation (TM), which focuses on an internally recited mantra, and, to my surprise, it helped too.

In fact, when I had less children and could practise twice a day without being interrupted with demands for cheese and *Octonauts*, it made me feel marvellous to the point of euphoria.

Because any creative thoughts had while TM-ing deserve full expression (according to me, not the woman who taught me, who said that a lot of what came out of my thinking during meditation should be cheerfully ignored), I now have a five-foot by five-foot bit of plyboard covered in carefully snipped-out magazine pictures – stuff like people hugging scary bears, and balloons, and good-looking people indulging in whimsical beach-staring, with sponge-painted trees and clouds over the top in hot pink.

Plus I made friends come to my house for a clothes-swap meet. Only five people couldn't think of an excuse to get out of it fast enough and had to sit around my lounge room while I maniacally forced them to try on clothes from my wardrobe that hadn't been in fashion since 1996, and only questionably then.

But I'll take that over locking myself in my room for weeks on end.

The management of my anxiety (and god how I despise the word 'management', it makes me feel like a bored public servant dealing with an employee I'm not allowed to fire) is broad.

If I'm home and I can feel the twinge of anxiety in my chest, I say, 'Sod your alcohol-as-avoidance defence', and I have a glass of wine.

If things get really bad and I have one of my (now rare) panic attacks that cannot be talked down or distracted, I take a beta blocker, which gets rid of the physical symptoms long enough for me to get my head straight again.

I run, I go to see friends, I ring my mum, who is still there whenever I need her to listen to me blurt out all the things I am panicked about.

Find the ones who love you, anxiety and all.

Now I'm older my anxiety is less well tolerated by many, less people want to help, like there is a pervasive feeling that I should be over it by now. That I am somehow choosing to be this way, as if anyone would. As I edge closer to forty I am less 'manic-pixie-dream-girl' and more 'sad-old-loony-nearing-pre-menopause'.

You can get away with being scatty and nervous and jumpy when you are cute or sexy, preferably both. But mania and anxiety when attached to eye bags and dust-filled ovaries are altogether less attractive. No one wants to save grandma from herself.

You'll still meet people who think you are putting your anxiety on, or that it isn't as bad as you seem to think because 'everyone gets worried'.

It doesn't matter what they think – we know the truth.

Much of my fury now is reserved for my son's fear and my inability to protect him. When I see Sam curl in on himself I want to rage at the universe and myself. I want to yell in my own face, 'A GOOD MOTHER WOULD BE ABLE TO HELP HIM, A GOOD MOTHER WOULD KNOW THE RIGHT WORDS TO SAY.'

Even with everything I have learned, anxiety wants to find the cracks to seep through, in fear and self-doubt.

When I was contracted to write this book, surely any journo's dream (the deal, not the subject matter), I visualised myself getting up every morning to run at 6 a.m. before sitting at my beautiful wooden desk (don't have one), music playing in the background (can't work our stereo), where the words and insights would flow from my fingers so quickly that I would scarcely be able to break for healthy lunches and afternoon meditation sessions. But instead of sitting down at my computer early in the morning, coffee at hand and fingernails neatly trimmed, I drove, mightily hungover, aimlessly around the streets for hours because I was too freaked out to start writing a book which, I was sure, would confirm to me and everybody else that I have no business writing a book of any kind.

The irony of getting anxiety about writing a book about getting rid of anxiety is not lost on me.

Yet here I am, at the end, book finished, and I can't believe I made it, and if you can't tell I am trying to find a clumsy parallel between writing this book and squashing anxiety then you might want to turn back to page one and start all over again.

If you haven't got time, though, I'll try to be a little clearer: the key is never giving up.

The key is recognising the nature of my anxiety. Your anxiety.

The key is understanding that our fears are not unique, cannot be ascribed with the truth we think they are deserving of because they are specific and detailed and must be true.

There is nothing unique about our fears – my fears; even the most bespoke are shared by others who may also feel as isolated and trapped, as defined by them as we do. This doesn't make them real.

The key is no more running away. The key is exploration. The key is acceptance.

The key is hope. Always hope.

And, finally, I need to challenge that deepest of beliefs. That anxiety is a part of me and that, without it, I will lose some quickness or humour or sensitivity – something I value. That the good in me is tied inextricably with the bad. That anxiety isn't just a part of me, that it *is* me.

Who am I without anxiety?

I find myself sitting calmly, heart beating normally, gut relaxed, and then wonder why I feel okay and the twinge begins and I feel, horrifyingly, almost reassured by its presence. I have had it for so long that I feel that it somehow looks after me.

Who am I without the pounding heart?

Without the hypervigilance?

Without the wired brain?

Without the nervous energy and self-deprecation and edge?

The primitive part of my mind whispers that *it* is the reason I am okay. The primitive part of my mind knows that anxiety is the guard dog, the watchtower. The primitive part of my mind niggles that if I let anxiety go and something bad happens, it will be my fault.

And yet. *And yet.*

Anxiety grips me, scares me, holds me in its clutches.

It is the blank look, the tears, the lost loves, the shame, the regret.

Anxiety is the fear of tomorrow, tonight, the next moment.

It is not keeping me safe, it is not stopping the bad things from happening.

It is the bad thing.

So I let it go. Let go of control and try to embrace the chaos and unpredictability and messiness and hurt. Because that is life. And letting go of anxiety is finding my peace with potential pain; calm in chaos; joy in surprises; appreciation of the beauty all around.

Because I have hope. I always have hope.

Acknowledgements

Mum and Dad – thanks for the advice, support, unconditional love (even after reading about semen) and round-the-clock childcare.

Sophie Hamley and Sophie Mayfield – for signing me up and talking me off multiple ledges.

Shane Rodgers and Deb Bogle – thank you for helping me find my first words.

Roy Eccleston – for believing there was a story worth telling in the first place.

Christine D and Emily S – for the wine and the whine.

Kel, Erika and Claire – no less important for being invisible friends.

Matt Pike – a lover of words who helped me find something to love in mine.

Laura Cooke-O'Connor, Simon Andrews and Dr Andrea Robertson – for the professional advice and sympathetic ears.

Dr Andrew Owen – for being the best kind of old-school doctor.

Quentin Kenihan – book-angst shared is book-angst halved, or something.

Colleagues Lynn, Lisa and Liz – for listening, laughing and letting me talk about myself a lot.

Gen, Heather, Kelly, Resh, Fitz, Brooke, Kate B and Kate G – for being the kind of friends who build you up and believe you can do ridiculous things.

And to Josh, Z and J – my eternal loves – thank you for loving all of me.

Endnotes

What is anxiety?

1 SANE Australia, Facts and Figures Factsheet, SANE Australia, viewed 16 February 2016, www.sane.org/mental-health-and-illness/facts-and-guides/facts-figures

Disgust

1 SJ Thorpe, SP Patel & LM Simonds, 'The relationship between disgust sensitivity, anxiety and obsessions', *Behaviour Research and Therapy*, vol. 41, no. 12, 2003, pp. 1397–1409.

2 GCL Davey, 'Disgust: the disease-avoidance emotion and its dysfunctions', *Philosophical Transactions of the Royal Society B*, vol. 366, issue 1583, 2011, pp. 3453–3465.

3 P Muris, B Mayer, M Borth & M Vos, 'Nonverbal and verbal transmission of disgust from mothers to offspring: effects on children's evaluation of a novel animal', *Behavior Therapy*, vol. 44, 2013, pp. 293–301.

4 SJ Thorpe, SP Patel & LM Simonds, *Behaviour Research and Therapy*, pp. 1397–1409.

5 GCL Davey, *Philosophical Transactions of the Royal Society B*, pp. 3453–3465.

6 P Gilbert & B Andrews, *Shame: interpersonal behaviour, psychopathology, and culture*, Oxford Press, New York, 1998.

7 GCL Davey, *Philosophical Transactions of the Royal Society B*, pp. 3453–3465.

8 W Taboas, R Ojserkis & D Mackay, 'Change in disgust reactions following cognitive-behavioural therapy for childhood anxiety disorders', *International Journal of Clinical and Health Psychology*, vol. 15, issue 1, 2015, pp. 1–7.

9 J Cisler, B Olatunji & J Lohr, 'Disgust, fear, and the anxiety disorders: a critical review', *Clinical Psychology Review*, vol. 29, 2009, pp. 34–46.

Epigenetics – The importance of ancestors

1 P Wirtz, S Elsenbruch, L Emini, K Rüdisüli, S Groessbauer & U Ehlert, 'Perfectionism and the cortisol response to psychosocial stress in men', *Psychosomatic Medicine*, vol. 69, issue 3, 2007, pp. 249–255.

2 I Skre, S Onstad, S Torgersen, S Lygren & E Kringlen, 'A twin study of DSM-III-R anxiety disorders', *Acta Psychiatra Scandinavica*, vol. 88, 1993, pp. 85–92.

3 K Northstone, J Golding, G Davey Smith, L Miller & M Pembrey, 'Prepubertal start of father's smoking and increased body fat in his sons: further characterisation of paternal transgenerational responses', *European Journal of Human Genetics*, vol. 22, 2014, pp. 1382–1386.

4 B Dias & K Ressler, 'Parental olfactory experience influences behaviour and neural structure in subsequent generations', *Nature Neuroscience*, vol. 117, no. 1, 2014, pp 89–99.

5 K Godfrey, A Sheppard, P Gluckman, K Lillycrop, G Burdge, C McLean & J Rodford, 'Epigenetic gene promoter methylation at birth is associated with child's later adiposity', *Diabetes*, vol. 60, no. 5, 2011, pp. 1528–1534.

6 R Yehuda, N Daskalakis, L Bierer, H Bader, T Klengel, F Holsboer & E Binder, 'Holocaust exposure induced intergenerational effects on FKBP5 methylation', *Biological Psychiatry*, PMID 26410355, DOI: 10.1016/j.biopsych.2015.08.005, 2015.

7 K Gudsnuk & F Champagne, 'Epigenetic Influence of Stress and the Social Environment', *ILAR Journal*, vol. 53, issue 3, 2012, pp. 279–288.

Water phobia, tummy aches and ritual

1 G Shelby, K Shirkey, A Sherman, J Beck, K Haman & A Shears, 'Functional abdominal pain in childhood and long-term vulnerability to anxiety disorders', *Pediatrics*, vol. 132, issue 3, 2013, pp. 475–482.

2 B Gholipour, 'Kids with Tummy Aches May Grow to Anxious Adults', *LiveScience*, viewed 16 February 2016, www.livescience. com/38806-kids-stomachaches-anxious-adults.html

3 B Gholipour, *LiveScience*.

4 D Eilam, R Izhar & J Mort, 'Threat detection: behavioral practices in animals and humans', *Neuroscience & Biobehavioural Reviews*. vol. 35, issue 4, 2011, pp. 999–1006.

Avoidance

1 H Trinder & P Salkovskis, 'Personally relevant intrusions outside the laboratory: long-term suppression increases intrusion', *Behaviour Research and Therapy*, vol. 32, issue 8, 1994, pp. 833–842.

2 A Boyes, 'Why Avoidance Coping is the Most Important Factor in Anxiety', *Psychology Today*, 2013, viewed 2 March 2016, www.psychologytoday.com/blog/in-practice/201303/ why-avoidance-coping-is-the-most-important-factor-in-anxiety

Positive negativity

1 J Norem, *The Positive Power of Negative Thinking*, Basic Books, New York, 2001.

2 J Norem, email interview with the author, 11 September 2015.

Health anxiety and emetophobia

1 M Overveld, P de Jong, M Peters, W van Hout & T Bouman, 'An internet-based study on the relation between disgust sensitivity and emetophobia', *Journal of Anxiety Disorders*, vol. 22, issue 3, 2008, pp. 524–531.

2 D Veale, P Murphy, N Ellison, N Kanakam & A Costa, 'Autobiographical memories of vomiting in people with a specific phobia of vomiting (emetophobia)', *Journal of Behavior Therapy and Experimental Psychiatry*, vol. 44, issue 1, 2012, pp. 14–20.

3 S Stossel, *My Age of Anxiety*, Random House, London, 2014.

4 L Saulsman, email interview with the author, 29 February 2016.

Performance anxiety

1   R May, *The Meaning of Anxiety*, Norton, New York, 2015.

Superstition and magical thinking

1   B Skinner, 'Superstition in the pigeon', *Journal of Experimental Psychology*, vol. 38, issue 2, 1948, pp. 168–172.
2   E Langer, 'The illusion of control', *Journal of Personality and Social Psychology*, vol. 32, issue 2, 1975, pp. 311–328.

Panic disorder and agoraphobia

1   P Skapinakis, G Lewis & S Davies, 'Panic disorder and subthreshold panic in the UK general population: epidemiology, comorbidity and functional limitation', *European Psychiatry*, vol. 26, no. 6, 2010, pp. 354–362.
2   Beyond Blue, The Facts Factsheet, viewed 2 March 2016, www.beyondblue.org.au/the-facts
3   P Ham, A Waters & M Oliver, 'Treatment of panic disorder', *American Family Physician*, vol. 71, no. 4, 2005, pp. 733–739.
4   J Rowney, Cleveland Clinic Centre for Continuing Education, 2004, viewed 2 March 2016, www.clevelandclinicmeded.com/medicalpubs/diseasemanagement/psychiatry-psychology/anxiety-disorder

Generalised anxiety disorder

1   Australian Bureau of Statistics, National Survey of Mental Health and Wellbeing, 2007, viewed 2 March 2016, www.abs.gov.au/ausstats
2   M Newman & S Llera, 'A novel theory of experiential avoidance in generalised anxiety disorder: a review and synthesis of research supporting a contrast avoidance model of worry', *Clinical Psychology Review*, vol. 31, issue 3, 2011, pp. 371–382.

Postnatal anxiety and depression

1   Perinatal Anxiety and Depression Australia, Factsheets, viewed 2 March 2016, www.panda.org.au/learning-with-panda/panda-resources/fact-sheets
2   C Chojenta, J Lucke, P Forder & D Loxton, 'Maternal health factors as risks for postnatal depression: a prospective longitudinal study', *PLoS One*, vol. 11, no. 1, 2016, pp. 1–9.

3 S Misri, P Reebye, M Corral & L Mills, 'The use of paroxetine and cognitive-behavioural therapy in postpartum depression and anxiety: a randomized controlled trial', *Journal of Clinical Psychiatry*, vol. 65, no. 9, 2004, pp. 1236–1241.

How to help the anxious child

1 N Zucker, W Copeland, L Franz, K Carpenter, L Keeling, A Angold & H Egger, 'Psychological and psychosocial impairment in preschoolers with selective eating', *Pediatrics*, vol. 136, no. 3, 2015, pp. 1–9.
2 F Orchard, P Cooper & C Creswell, 'Interpretation and expectations among mothers of children with anxiety disorders: associations with maternal anxiety disorder', *Depression and Anxiety*, vol. 32, 2015, pp. 99–107.
3 The Mental Health of Children and Adolescents, 2015, viewed 2 March 2016, www.health.gov.au
4 V Cobham, email interview with the author, 24 February 2016.
5 J Hudson, K Lester, C Lewis, M Tropeano, C Cresswell, D Collier, P Cooper, H Lyneham, T Morrie, R Rapee & S Roberts, 'Predicting outcomes following cognitive behaviour therapy in child anxiety disorders: the influence of genetic, demographic and clinical information', *The Journal of Child Psychology and Psychiatry*, vol. 54, no. 10, 2013, pp. 1086–1094.
6 S Andrews, email interview with the author, 25 February 2016.
7 J Hudson & H Dodd, 'Informing early intervention: preschool predictors of anxiety disorders in middle childhood', *PLoS ONE*, vol. 7, issue 8, 2012, pp 1–7.

The future

1 E Le Chateliar, T Nielsen, J Qin, E Prifti, F Hildebrand, G Falony, M Almedia, M Arumuguam & J Batto, 'Richness of human gut microbiome correlates with metabolic markers', *Nature*, vol. 500, 2013, pp. 541–546.
2 J Molloy, K Allen, F Collier, M Tang, A Ward & P Vuillermin, 'The potential link between gut microbiota and IgE-mediated food allergy in early life', *International Journal of Environmental Research and Public Health*, vol. 10, issue 12, 2013, pp. 7235–7256.
3 J Andrews, email interview with the author, 17 November 2015.

4   A Mikocka-Walus, email interview with the author, 17 November
    2015.
5   K Lebron-Milad & M Milad, 'Low estradiol levels: a vulnerability
    factor for the development of posttraumatic stress disorder', *Biological
    Psychiatry*, vol. 72, issue 1, 2012, pp. 6–7.
6   J Levine, I Timinsky, T Vishne, T Dwolatzky, S Roitman, Z Kaplan,
    M Kotler, B Sela & B Spivak, 'Elevated serum homocysteine levels
    in male patients with PTSD', *Depression and Anxiety*, vol. 25, no. 11,
    2008, pp. 154–157.
7   S Gilbody, S Lewis & T Lightfoot, 'Methylenetetrahydrofolate
    reductase (MTHFR) genetic polymorphisms and psychiatric disorders:
    a HuGE review', *American Journal of Epidemiology*, vol. 165, issue 1,
    2007, pp. 1–13.
8   C Kelly, A McDonnell, T Johnston, C Mulholland, S Cooper,
    D McMaster, A Evans & A Whitehead, 'The MTHFR C677T
    polymorphism is associated with depressive episodes in patients from
    Northern Ireland', *Journal of Psychopharmacology*, vol. 18, no. 4, 2004,
    pp. 567–571.
9   C Gokcen, N Kocak & A Pekgor, 'Methylenetetrahydrofolate
    reductase gene polymorphisms in children with attention deficit
    hyperactivity disorder', *International Journal of Medical Sciences*, vol. 8,
    no. 7, 2011, pp. 523–528.
10 R Frye, J Sequeira, E Quadros, E James & D Rossignol, 'Cerebral
    folate receptor autoantibodies in autism spectrum disorder', *Molecular
    Psychiatry*, vol. 18, 2013, pp. 369–381.

Resources

Australian resources

Beyond Blue
beyondblue.org.au

Headspace
headspace.org.au

Kids Helpline (up to twenty-five years)
kidshelpline.com.au

Lifeline
lifeline.org.au

Mind Health Connect
mindhealthconnect.org.au

Mindspot
mindspot.org.au

PANDA
panda.org.au

Reach Out
au.reachout.com

Sane Australia
sane.org

New Zealand resources

Anxiety New Zealand Trust
anxiety.org.nz

Headspace
headspace.org.nz

Healthline
health.govt.nz

Lifeline Aotearoa
lifeline.org.nz

Mental Health Education & Resource Centre
mherc.org.nz

Mental Health Foundation of New Zealand
mentalhealth.org.nz

Youthline
youthline.co.nz